FROM PUSHKIN

TO MAYAKOVSKY

Janko Lavrin

FROM PUSHKIN TO MAYAKOVSKY

A Study in the Evolution of a Literature

GREENWOOD PRESS, PUBLISHERS
WESTPORT, CONNECTICUT

Originally published in 1948
by Sylvan Press Ltd., London

First Greenwood Reprinting 1971

Library of Congress Catalogue Card Number 72-114540

SBN 8371-4741-7

Printed in the United States of America

CONTENTS

Prefatory Note

THE TITLE CHOSEN FOR THIS BOOK IS NOT ARBITRARY. The period between Pushkin and Mayakovsky represents all that has been truly creative in Russian literature and culture during some hundred years in which Russia, conscious of her backwardness, tried to achieve what other nations had achieved in the course of several centuries. No one could give an adequate picture of those achievements merely by analysing the work of a dozen individual authors—least of all in a book of this size. All one can hope to do is to indicate some of the basic elements and dispositions typical of the character, the growth and the crisis of Russian literature during that span of time.

This is why the chapters of the book are equally divided between poetry and prose. As for the poets, Pushkin, Blok and Mayakovsky are known at least by name in this country. The names of Lermontov, Tyutchev, Nekrasov and Esenin, on the other hand, sound as yet unfamiliar to the English ear, although no student of Russia and of her literature can ignore them. Things are different with the prose writers. Such towering figures as Tolstoy and Dostoevsky are so well known all the world over that one is justified in limiting oneself to some of their characteristics only. In the case of Chekhov it is above all his dramatic work and technique that come here into consideration ; whereas Leskov, Gorky and Andreyev are worth discussing both for their intrinsic and their symptomatic values.

Much of the material here presented was given, on various occasions, in the form of lectures to my students, or else in the form of prefaces, introductory essays, comments, etc., in various editions, notably in *Pushkin's Poems*, translated by Walter Morison (The Prague Press, Allen & Unwin) and *Petersburg Stories* (Lindsay Drummond) and *Gogol's Tales* (The Sylvan Press). The poems and passages quoted have been taken from several editions, mentioned in each case separately in the text. My thanks and acknowledgments are due to the publishers and translators of those works. I also express my sincere gratitude to Walter Morison and to my colleagues Professor V. de Sola Pinto and Professor R. M. Hewitt, who translated several poems for this particular edition.

J. L.

ONE

Alexander Pushkin

I

THE RAPID RISE OF RUSSIAN LITERATURE FROM ITS modest beginnings to the status of a literary great power still remains as puzzling as it is fascinating. Having started, in the first half of the eighteenth century, under the sign of imported pseudo-classicism, it gradually assimilated Western influences in such a way as to be able to assert in the next century its own originality and to become, in something like fifty or sixty years, one of the richest and most stimulating literatures in the world. The man whose work gave a mighty impetus to this process was Alexander Sergeyevich Pushkin (1799-1837).

Pushkin is a strange and in some respects unique phenomenon. Under one of the most tyrannical regimes in Europe he knew how to preserve his creative freedom and, in spite of all the obstacles, to crystallise the irrepressible vitality and *joie de vivre* of a belated

Renaissance figure into works of imperishable harmony and beauty. A Russian to his very core, he yet absorbed organically the literary and cultural heritage —in fact, the entire humanistic tradition—of the West and grafted it upon his native country as part and parcel of its own inner life. In addition to being the greatest national poet of Russia, he thus became the principal link between the literature of his own country and the literatures of Europe, notably that of England. He not only provided a brilliant conclusion to the period which preceded him in Russia, but indicated, in his own creations, that kind of synthesis between Russia and Europe which could serve as a pointer to the future. In spite of that, Pushkin is probably the only first-rate genius whose reputation outside Russia rests on credit rather than on actual acquaintance with his work. The fact that he is a great poet and, in a way, the founder of modern Russian literature is taken of course for granted. Nevertheless, a European ignorant of the Russian language and culture can hardly understand what the name of Pushkin means to a Russian and what his name stands for.

This drawback is further increased by a lack of adequate translations. And Pushkin still remains one of the most difficult poets to translate—difficult mainly on account of his uncanny ease, obviousness (he is perhaps the greatest genius of the obvious), and simplicity. Equally uncanny was his flair for the *mot juste*, for the right inflection, as well as for that orchestration of sounds, rhymes and rhythms the harmony of which, inseparable from the emotional and the logical meaning of the words, he always worked out with matchless clarity. Few poets indeed have known how to extract the full value out of each word with that Hellenic instinct for art that conceals art which is one of Pushkin's primary qualities. In his poems each word, each image, seems to be born out of another with that inevitability which excludes anything artificial, forced and laboured. And the more perfect and disciplined the result, the stronger is the impression of spontaneity. The texture of his verse, too, is so individual that it is impossible to confuse it with that of anybody else. He may and often does use several parallel themes in one and the same poem, yet he organises them in such a balanced polyphonic manner as to make the content utterly indivisible from its rhythmical and verbal pattern. The economy, the sparkling lucidity and precision, which as a boy Pushkin had learned from the French poets (including Voltaire and Parny), he later combined with his own realistic sense, as well as with that broad perception of life which made him compare himself, in one of his lyrics, with the echoes, reproducing all the sounds and vibrations around even if the echoes remain unanswered.

When cries of beasts the forests fill,
The thunder rolls, the trumpets shrill,
A maiden sings behind the hill,
To every sound
Responsive, sudden echoes thrill
The air around.

They hear the thunder's roaring glee,
The stormy sobbing of the sea,
The shouts of shepherds on the lea,
And answers find,
Themselves unanswered.—How like thee,
*Poetic mind.**

Intensely human and all of this world, Pushkin "echoed" everything in terms of visual images and symbols, that is, of concrete reality. However intimate his personal experiences, he knew how to sublimate them, especially in his matchless love-lyrics, by means of his "shorthand" realism into things of beauty the purport of which is far above the merely personal. In his poetry there is no gap between the physical and the spiritual planes, between "soul" and "body." Instead of being hostile, the two are mutually complementary and, in fact, inseparable. No matter how impulsive, passionate, even turbulently passionate he may have been as a man, as a poet he remained to the end one of the most balanced geniuses in world literature—in some respects even more balanced than Goethe. His was not a static, but a dynamic balance which made him experience life as an *élan vital*, as a tense perpetual movement. Feeling at home in this world, he adopted that affirmative attitude which accepts all life—whether "happy" or "unhappy"—provided it is really intense. What he

* Translated, together with the other quotations in the first three sections, by Walter Morison. English readers may be interested to know that the theme of this exquisite lyric was inspired by an English poem, *The Sea-Shore Echo*, by Barry Cornwall.

hated was sham-life, camouflaged by all sorts of respectable labels. It was for this reason that he affirmed life in its entirety, with its joys and sorrows, even the most tragic sorrows. Such acceptance is perhaps best expressed in his well-known *Elegy*, full of readiness to face any adversities without saying *no* to existence.

The frenzied merriment of misspent years
Like wakening from wine my spirit sears:
Like wine, the poignant imprints of past pain
Grow stronger in me as in years they gain.
My path is sombre ; fraught with toil and sorrow
The storm-encompassed ocean of tomorrow.

And yet, my friends, I do not ask for death ;
Life I desire, for pain and contemplation.
I know I shall be stirred by pleasure's breath
'Mid all my grief, and care, and agitation.
Again at times with melody I'll throb,
My fancy's fruit again will make me sob ;
And maybe, as my last sad days decline,
Love with a farewell smile on me will shine.

II

PUSHKIN'S APPETITE FOR LIFE WAS SO STRONG INDEED that on a purely human plane and amidst ordinary circumstances he was, despite his incredible sense of measure, often swayed by weaknesses and vagaries the causes of which may, perhaps, be traced to his exotic ancestry. Whereas on his father's side he came of an aristocratic Russian stock six hundred years old, his maternal great-grandfather had been an Abyssinian princeling, bought in the slave market at Constantinople and sent as a present to Peter the Great, who took good care of his education and his subsequent career. Pushkin's own parents were rather commonplace, without any particular talents or distinctions. Besides, he saw little of them, and the only person for whom he felt genuine attachment in his childhood was his old nurse Arina. That lovable peasant-woman was actually destined to form something of a bridge between the poet and the people. As a boy of twelve he was sent to the newly opened *Lycée* or privileged boarding school at Tsarskoye Selo (now called Pushkin), where the atmosphere was so much to his liking that, years afterwards, he always commemorated in verse the opening day—October 19th. One of these poems, *October 19th*, 1825, ranks among his finest and best-known creations. Its first two stanzas may serve as an example of what the whole of it (written in exile) is like:

The autumn wood casts off its crimson gown,
The faded field is silvered o'er with frost,
The sun peers forth, a sad, reluctant ghost,
And hurriedly behind the hill goes down.
Burn brightly, pine-logs, in my lonely cell;
And thou, O wine-cup, that in autumn rains
Dost comfort so, in my sad heart instil
A brief oblivion of bitter pains.

How sad I am, no friend to comfort me,
With whom my sorrows I might solve in drink,
Whose trusty hand in my hand I might link
And wish him all his days felicity.
I drink alone ; in vain my fancy calls
To visit me the friends of former years ;
No pleasure I await ; no footstep falls
With sweet familiar ring upon my ears.

The five or six years of Pushkin's schooling at the *Lycée* were responsible for the enduring friendships which he alludes to in the two verses quoted. But those were also the years which coincided with one of the most eventful and promising eras in modern Russian history. The younger generation, which had witnessed Russia's victory over Napoleon in 1812, could not but expect a better future for their country. The two basic evils of Russia—serfdom and autocracy —weighed heavily on all those who hoped for the eventual triumph of justice and freedom ; but as the years passed things only became worse under the jackboot of reaction. Still, the ideas bequeathed by the French Revolution could not be entirely suppressed even in Russia, where a considerable portion of the young aristocrats aimed at reforms corresponding to the more liberal spirit of the age. Disappointed in their hopes, these liberals found an outlet in secret societies. Finally, on December 14th, 1825, an open revolt broke out against the new Tsar Nicholas I, the brother of the deceased Alexander I. It was engineered chiefly by the officers of the Guards—all of them sincere patriots, anxious to turn Russia into a free constitutional country. Unfortunately, their organisation was so bad that the venture ended in a *débâcle.* Five of the most prominent "Decembrists" (as they were called henceforth) were hanged. The rest, one hundred and twenty in all, were sent to Siberia. Yet in spite of its failure, this revolt from above became a landmark in the social history of Russia and a source of inspiration for all the subsequent fighters for freedom.

Pushkin, who belonged to the same section of the landed gentry, had a number of friends among the "Decembrists" and was in fact their favourite bard. Quite a few of his earlier verses were saturated with the spirit of rebellion. One of them, *The Dagger*, he dedicated to the German student Sand, who in 1819 stabbed to death the notorious reactionary and spy (in the Russian service) Kotzebue, otherwise known as the most popular German playwright of that period. Sand's instrument of revenge, the dagger—a "secret punisher of Freedom's rape"—is addressed by Pushkin in terms such as these :

Like dart from Hell, or bolt by gods released,
Thy silent blade gleams in the tyrant's eyes ;
He trembles, as around he spies
For death amidst the feast.

Where'er he be, thy point seeks out his sin:
On land, on sea, in temple, in the field,
On passion's couch, among his kin,
By secret locks concealed.

After the total defeat of the rebels, Pushkin's revolutionary zeal was temporarily cooled down, yet his allegiance to the cause of freedom never faltered. In the very heyday of the "leaden regime," imposed upon Russia by Nicholas I, he wrote his revolutionary *Message to Siberia* (addressed to his "Decembrist" friends), which ends with the promise that eventually—

will the heavy fetters fall,
The prison crumble ; freedom's words
Will greet you by the dungeon wall,
Your brothers bear you swords.

III

THE TRAGEDY OF FRUSTRATION AMONG THOSE YOUNGER intellectuals of the gentry class, who at the time were the guardians of Russian culture, can be imagined. Yet by some paradox of history it was in the years of reaction and oppression that Russia passed through her "golden age" of poetry. The starting point was the publication of Pushkin's *Ruslan and Ludmila* (1820), which brought him national fame. Here a fantastically romantic theme is treated with the classical discipline, detachment and the sparkling wit typical of the eighteenth century. Pushkin's gaily sensuous acceptance of life is equally reminiscent of that easy-going age. But when the sprightly epic appeared its author was already in exile. Because of some biting epigrams he had been ordered, in the spring of the same year, to leave Petersburg for the South of Russia whence he made a journey to the Caucasus and the Crimea. He was then transferred to Kishinev in Bessarabia (where he lived much as he pleased) ; from there to the more civilised Odessa ; and finally, in the summer of 1824, he was ordered to go to his mother's estate, Mikhailovskoye, in the North.

This compulsory absence from Petersburg, apart from having prevented Pushkin from joining the December revolt, gave him enough leisure to deepen his literary interests and to bring his genius to maturity. The products of his exile were amazingly good and varied, however painful his loneliness may have been at times. But in the autumn of 1826 the poet was summoned by the Tsar's special courier, to Moscow, where the coronation festivities were in full swing. Nicholas I received Pushkin amiably, pardoned his past "transgressions," and cunningly offered to be the only censor of his future writings.

The Tsar's intention may have been to turn the greatest Russian genius into a glorifier of the reactionary regime. In this he failed, although, beguiled by his assumed friendliness, Pushkin became well-disposed towards him personally—at least for the time being. The poet's entanglements with the Tsar and with the Court, however involuntary on his part, assumed a few years later a character which was bound to interfere with the whole of his existence and even led to his premature death. It all started after his marriage (in 1831) to the beautiful but not over-intelligent Natalia Goncharova. Natalia was graciously (too graciously) noticed by the Tsar himself. In order to enable her to attend the exclusive court balls Nicholas in 1834 made her husband a "gentleman of the chamber"—an office suitable for a youth of eighteen, but hardly for a man of thirty-five and a great poet into the bargain. It was obviously an affront, which Pushkin resented but could do nothing about.

Meanwhile, the queue of Natalia's admirers kept growing, the Tsar himself being at the head of it. The most persistent of these was a certain d'Anthès—a French refugee with a commission in the Guards. Having been "adopted" by the Dutch Ambassador, Baron Heeckeren (notorious as a pervert and intriguer), he was able to cut a society figure. For some reason Heeckeren himself did all he could to bring about a liaison between Natalia and his rather smart "son." Gossip and slander took their usual course. Disgusted with the "gilded rabble," Pushkin thought of escaping from it all to Mikhailovskoye, where he hoped to live in his own way—

. . . called to render
Account to no one; free to serve and suit
Oneself alone; not forced to bend one's neck,
One's conscience, thoughts to livery and power,
At liberty to wander here and there
And savour all the beauty of creation,
Before the fruits of art and inspiration
Swoon in a speechless spasm of delight—
There's happiness indeed, and human right.

But Natalia would have none of it. She was too much fascinated by the noisy glitter of society. Besides, it was made clear to the poet that the Tsar himself would be displeased by such an "ungrateful" move. So Pushkin stayed on—he had to. The intrigues, with all the inevitable scandal and gossip, gradually reached such proportions that he found it necessary to defend his wife's honour as well as his own. On January 27th, 1837, a duel between him and d'Anthès took place. Pushkin was mortally wounded and died two days later in his thirty-eighth year.

IV

DESPITE SUCH A SHORT LIFE, PUSHKIN LEFT A GREAT literary heritage in verse and in prose. In both he showed a rare capacity for adapting himself to others in order to adapt them to himself. He experienced a number of literary influences, without however succumbing to any of them. Having absorbed them instead, he thereby increased the wide range and also the peculiar originality of his own genius. The strongest influences came from England and were connected with the names of Byron, Shakespeare and Sir Walter Scott respectively. Yet all of them, while acting as powerful stimuli, were remodelled by Pushkin in his own image.

Pushkin's Byronic period came after the earlier spell of French influences and was responsible for his four

Byronic tales in verse, all of them written between 1821 and 1824 : *The Prisoner of the Caucasus*, *The Fountain of Bakhchisaray*, *The Robber Brothers*, and *The Gipsies*, of which only the second one is entirely romantic. The other three, for all their romantic motifs, abound in that terse classical realism which was one of the basic features of Pushkin's genius. True enough, in *The Prisoner of the Caucasus* and in *The Gipsies* he introduced into Russian literature the uprooted Childe Harold type, but even this essentially romantic hero is shown in a realistic setting. Later, in *The Gipsies*, he debunked not only his egotism, but also the fallacy of any Rousseauesque-Byronic "back to nature" tendency, that is, back to a more primitive state of consciousness which has already been left behind by history and civilisation. Finally, Pushkin debunked the Byronic poseur, fashionable in those days also on the banks of the Neva, in his famous *Evgeny Onegin* (1823-31).

This "novel in verse," as Pushkin himself calls it, is his central and in many respects most typical creation. It was in it that he overcame Byron on Byron's own ground. His first intention seems to have been to write a satirical equivalent of Byron's *Don Juan*. But having probably realised that Russian censorship would never allow him to publish a satire after his own heart, he wrote a lyrical "novel" instead, in which such a romantic prig as Onegin was transferred to the Russian countryside in its true setting of the 1820's.

The very contrast between the unsophisticated warmth and simplicity of the countryfolk on the one hand, and the *blasé* child of Petersburg society on the other, was enough to explain why Onegin remained quite the same poseur in his inherited manor as he had been before in the capital. His cold priggishness had become so much his second nature that he could not divest himself of it even when coming across the profound love on the part of Tatyana—a shy, inexperienced product of the country-house, yet potentially full of strength and character. In her naïve sincerity it was she who first confessed to Onegin her love for him, and this *faux pas* was itself enough to make the Petersburg dandy wince. With a few commonplaces to the effect that he is so disappointed with life as to be unable to love anyone, he returns her the letter she had, with such trepidation, sent to him. After months of boredom and ennui, during which Onegin kills in a stupid duel his only friend, he—like Childe Harold—spends a few years in travelling, and finally returns to the "high life" in Petersburg. There he meets Tatyana once again ; this time a mature married woman, admired by all as one of the most charming and dignified members of that rather exclusive circle. Now it is Onegin who falls in love with her and, in his turn, sends her letters which remain unanswered. When, in a fit of despair, he personally confesses to her his feelings, she acknowledges with firm candour that she still loves him but intends to remain faithful to her husband, and she means it. So in the end a note of frustration creeps into Onegin's fate which, despite his posing as a "Muscovite in Childe Harold's cloak," started a whole series of truly "superfluous men" in Russian fiction. However slender the plot of this "novel in verse" may be, its art remains supreme from the first to the last line. And its realistic background—the life and atmosphere in the 20's—is depicted so well that Pushkin's first great critic, Belinsky, wrote : "In *Onegin* we see a poetic picture of the whole of Russian society in one of the most interesting phases of its development. *Onegin* can be called an encyclopaedia of Russian life, and a national work in the highest degree." Written in the special "Onegin" stanzas (in four-footed iambics and consisting of fourteen lines), it lends itself to all sorts of moods, and sparkles like champagne in sunshine.

Some of Pushkin's other narrative poems, such as the humorous *Count Nulin* (its theme is in the style of the eighteenth century *contes*) and *The Little House in Kolomna*, are entirely realistic. The latter is even confined to lower middle-class characters, which was something of an innovation. Different in plane and treatment are, however, *Poltava* and *The Bronze Horseman*. Both of them deal with the larger destinies of Russia, while dwelling at the same time, each in its own way, on the "super-human" aspects of Peter the Great. *Poltava* is a torso of a national epic in the truest sense of this word, and is magnificent precisely as a torso. It combines two themes: the conflict between Russia and Sweden—at that time the most powerful maritime state in the North ; and the tragedy of Maria Kochubey who had fallen in love with the aged Mazepa, a secret ally of the Swedish King Charles XII. Enticed far into Southern Russia, the Swedes and the treacherous Mazepa were beaten at Poltava (1709)—a victory which made Russia an indisputable European power. The appearance of Peter I among his soldiers during the battle of Poltava is one of the best passages of descriptive poetry even in Pushkin's works.

The Bronze Horseman, commonly regarded as the greatest poem ever written in Russian, marks the height of Pushkin's poetic realism passing into the symbolic. The climax of the poem is the matchless picture of the flood of Petersburg in 1824, which caused incredible havoc and loss of life. Evgeny, an insignificant young *déclassé*, saves his life by clinging to the lions on the porch of the Senate House opposite the bronze monument of Peter the Great, the founder of the imperial city. Later he learns that his bride has perished in the disaster and is so crushed by it that he loses his reason. A deranged vagrant, he wanders in the city for weeks. One night he stops in the Senate Square before Peter's statue and vaguely recollects all that has happened in the accursed city whose founder now surges there like a demon on horseback. The madman flings curses at him and suddenly raises his fists. But here, in his dim mind, the bronze statue seems to have reared. Frightened, Evgeny begins to run through the cobbled streets, all the time hearing the clatter of bronze hoofs behind him. It is not his business to question whether Peter, in his designs for Russia's destiny, had any moral right to disregard the happiness of thousands of little men. Or, perhaps, it is! Pushkin only asks, but he does so with all the artistic power at his disposal.

ALEXANDER PUSHKIN

V

WHILE RETAINING THE PATTERN OF THE BYRONIC TALE in verse, Pushkin transcended Byron and only took from him what he needed for his own creative purposes. In a similar manner he underwent the influence of Shakespeare, the principal result of which was his drama, *Boris Godunov*—now known all the world over because of Moussorgsky's opera under the same title. Written at Mikhailovskoye in 1825, *Boris Godunov* was the first Shakespearian play in Russian literature. Pushkin took the subject matter from the "troubled period" at the end of the sixteenth and the beginning of the seventeenth centuries, when the pretender False Dimitry rose (with the help of the Poles) against the ruler Godunov—the supposed murderer of the real Tsarevich Dimitry and heir to Ivan the Terrible. He modelled this work, written in the five-footed iambic and in blank verse, on "our Father Shakespeare" largely in order to counteract the sterile pseudo-classic plays which still lingered on and even dominated the Russian stage. The result was not so much a play made all of a piece as an ably dramatised chronicle, in which (in spite of its title) the Pretender rather than Boris Godunov is the actual hero. While paying much attention to the "convincingness of situations and naturalness of the dialogue," Pushkin yet displayed a surprising sense of history. No less surprising was his understanding of the epoch concerned, not to mention his treatment of human characters and his great variety of dramatic scenes, in which he always achieved a maximum of effect by a minimum of means. The play itself was based on the pattern of Shakespeare's "Histories," but its condensed dialogue could only have been written by Pushkin.

Boris Godunov was not his only contribution to the dramatic literature of Russia. The four miniature plays, which he finished in the autumn of 1830, are small in size but big in artistic value. And here, too, English stimuli were at work. It was Barry Cornwall's now forgotten *Dramatic Scenes* that suggested to Pushkin the idea of writing his own series of "little tragedies." One of these, *The Feast at the Time of Plague*, was actually taken from John Wilson's *The City of the Plague* (1816) and translated, or rather paraphrased, into a Russian masterpiece in blank verse. Pushkin intended to write at least ten such miniature plays but finished only four. Each of these deals with one of the cardinal human passions: In *Mozart and Salieri* it is envy; in *The Miser Knight*—avarice and will to power; in *The Stone Guest* (Pushkin's own interpretation of the Don Juan motif) it is carnal lust; while the scene taken from *The Feast at the Time of Plague* is worked out so as to stress man's defiance in the very teeth of death.

Knowing well that all these themes had been widely used in European literature before him, Pushkin decided to tackle them not in order to repeat what had been said already, but to show them in a new light and from a new angle, in which he fully succeeded. But even in these miniature plays he shaped, again under the influence of Shakespeare, such complex characters as the Hamlet-like Salieri (the supposed poisoner of Mozart in the first of the four "little tragedies"), or the hero of *The Miser Knight*, so different from Molière's *Harpagon*, and interesting enough to have inspired, later on, the "idea" of Dostoevsky's novel *A Raw Youth.* He is like a Rothschild in a beggar's garb, and this makes him the more aware of his paradoxical power as one can judge by the end of his famous monologue in the cellar, amidst his coffers stuffed with ducats:

What does not own my sway? I, like some demon,
From here can dominate the universe.
I have but to wish. Palaces rise straightway,
And through the thickets of my glorious gardens
Fair nymphs go running in a merry crowd.
The Muses bring their tribute to my feet.
Free Genius is my slave and works for me,
Virtue and Toil, labouring sleeplessly,
Will humbly wait on me for recompense.
I shall but whistle and submissively
Will bloodstained Crime come crawling to my feet,
Timidly lick my hand, look in my eyes,
And read in them the signal of my will.
All shall be subject to me, I to nothing.
Out-stripping all desires I shall know peace.
I understand my power ; this knowledge
*Will be enough for me**

Pushkin's not entirely finished poetic play *Rusalka* (*The Water-Fairy*) can only be mentioned in passing. Here the central idea of retribution is intertwined with

* Translated by V. de Sola Pinto and W. Marshall.

Russian folk-lore, the spirit and the flavour of which he had splendidly rendered in his *Fairy-Tales* (*Skazki*) in verse, thus making an important *rapprochement* between literature and folk-lore.

VI

IN ADDITION TO HIS POETIC ACTIVITIES PUSHKIN WAS A pioneer of modern Russian prose. Here, too, as in poetry and the drama, he acted as a creative intermediary between English and Russian literatures. This time it was Sir Walter Scott who served as a stimulus for Pushkin's bigger narratives: *The Negro of Peter the Great* (unfinished), *Dubrovsky*, and *A Captain's Daughter*.

The first of these was to deal with Pushkin's Abyssinian maternal great-grandfather, Hannibal. Pushkin never went beyond the initial five chapters, but even within so small a compass he gave a fine picture of early eighteenth-century manners, as well as a full-size portrait of Peter the Great in his homelier and more human moods. *Dubrovsky* (not quite completed either) is based on a romantic plot, its central figure being a polished young gentleman turned brigand in order to avenge the wrongs done to his father by a feudal neighbour. The agitated incidents, slightly reminiscent at times of *The Bride of Lammermoor*, are set against a very realist background of the uncouth provincial gentry under the reign of Catherine II. Pushkin's principal work in prose, *A Captain's Daughter*, depicts the same period but on a bigger scale. Its subject-matter is the rising of the Ural Cossacks against Catherine II under the leadership of the illiterate peasant Pugachov, who gave himself out for the supposedly escaped Tsar Peter III (Catherine's "liquidated" husband), and threatened for a while a large portion of the central and lower Volga area. The narrative is much shorter than any of the Waverley Novels, and its style, modelled on the disciplined eighteenth-century prose, is enlivened by Pushkin's inimitable touch and inflection. A somewhat similar result might have been expected if one of Scott's novels had been written or rewritten, say, by Jane Austen. The whole of it has the character of a "family chronicle" narrated in the first person by a young nobleman whose fate became strangely involved with that of Pugachov and of his semi-Asiatic *Jacquerie*. Pushkin's research into the events described in this novel are recorded in his excellent *History of Pugachov's Rebellion*, which he began with his studies in the State archives and completed on a journey to the regions concerned.

Among his other writings in prose *The Tales of Belkin* and *The Queen of Spades* enjoy a deservedly high reputation. The five tales supposed to have been told by the "late Ivan Petrovich Belkin"—a simple, pathetic, yet somewhat comic figure—are reduced to their "naked" essentials, while yet skilfully preserving the narrator's tone and manner. One of these tales, *The Posting-Station Master*, exercised a considerable influence upon subsequent narratives (beginning with Gogol's *Greatcoat*) in so far as it definitely sanctioned the insignificant "little man" in Russian fiction. Besides, the would-be narrator Belkin himself is such a "little man," and his touching comicality becomes even more pronounced when we meet him, once again, as the compiler of Pushkin's unfinished satire on the serfdom system in *A History of the Village Goryukhino*.

Quite an amazing example of Pushkin's prose is his story *The Queen of Spades*, in which his art of the "naked word" is displayed to even better advantage than in his other prose works. A fantastic Hoffmannesque anecdote about a gambler, who in a mysterious way obtains the secret of winning at cards a large sum of money but loses the whole of it at his last stake and goes mad, is here worked out with incredible economy and detachment. The tale is moreover permeated with the atmosphere of that "irrational" Petersburg which was subsequently taken up and further developed by Dostoevsky. Last but not least, Pushkin's prose style scintillates also in his letters—the finest in Russian literature.

VII

WHEN ALL IS SAID AND DONE, PUSHKIN SEEMS TO REFUTE our current ideas about a "Russian" genius. It would be futile to look in him for any morbid introspection, or even for the passionate inner questing typical of

Gogol, Dostoevsky and Tolstoy. As an artist, at any rate, he was so harmonious and balanced that he is frequently referred to as a Hellene of the North. It was the broadness as well as the sanity of his genius that made him so universal. This enabled him to graft his universality of a late humanist upon the literature of Russia and make the latter a most creative part of European literature as a whole. Having brought all the previous literary achievements of his country to a conclusion, he thus opened up new possibilities, the consequences of which were far-reaching. There is not a single literary *genre* in which he did not excel or produce something memorable. And the number of new themes which he introduced helped to enlarge the area of Russian literature beyond all recognition. It was he, too, who directed it towards that simple yet monumental realism which became one of its most prominent characteristics in the second half of the nineteenth century.

Finally, in spite of his being the climax of the gentry culture in Russia, Pushkin helped to impart to the literature of his country a decidedly democratic, humanistic-democratic, and, in his early period, even revolutionary trend. He was, moreover, the first Russian poet who was read by all strata, from the highest to the lowest. And when modern literature, in the course of its growth, began to differentiate into a number of currents and "isms," Pushkin was accepted as the standard of literary values and also as a symbol of cultural continuity up to our own day.

"Pushkin is our all," said Apollon Grigoryev—one

of the highly intelligent Russian critics in the middle of the last century. And Pushkin's work, far from having aged since then, is still as vital as ever before. He is the most widely read classic in Russian, and the day is perhaps not far distant when he will be read as a universal classic also outside his own country.

TWO

Nikolai Gogol

I

WHEN PUSHKIN DIED, IN 1837, THERE WERE QUITE A few poets left to foster the growth of a literature which now rested on firm foundations of its own. Baratynsky—a prominent member of the Pushkin *pléiade*—wrote some of his best things after 1837, whereas the vigorous genius of Lermontov was just then in the ascendant. Yet the interest in poetry, as well as the high standard of craftsmanship, typical of the Pushkin era, from the 'forties onwards was on the decline. As a compensation, a mighty wave of prose set in, and the leadership in Russian letters now fell upon the shoulders of the greatest prose-writer of that period, Nikolai Vasilyevich Gogol (1809-1852), who, in almost every way, was a strange contrast to Pushkin. Whereas Pushkin marked the apex of the gentry period in Russian culture, Gogol's creative activities coincided with the early formation of the intelligentsia, in which

the voice of the educated "commoners" asserted itself through the critic Belinsky (1811-48). Mentally and temperamentally, the two were poles apart. Pushkin, who was a classical realist even in his romantic works, felt at home in this world, however much he may have clashed with some of its aspects. His genius was one of serene clarity and simplicity. Gogol, on the other hand, was so maladjusted and as though frightened of what he saw that he never felt at ease with the surrounding reality, and this attitude came out most conspicuously in his peculiar realism. Primitive, archaically primitive at times, but never simple, he became in fact the first enigmatic figure in modern Russian literature—a puzzled questioner for whom writing was a process of self-examination, self-defence and catharsis in one. Hence the two alternatives opened to Gogol the artist. One was escapist, and the other searchingly as well as aggressively realistic. It was with the first that he started his literary career, but he finished it with the second. This was however logical, since the two attitudes can be complementary to each other.

A disappointed and frustrated idealist of Gogol's stamp, who is haunted by life to such an extent as to be unable to find a shelter even in escapist romanticism, may in the end turn art itself into a "realistic" weapon for self-defence. And the greater his romantic rancour against the reality he is unable either to accept or to alter, the stronger will be his realism of indictment. His bitter laughter will be a revenge upon reality which he will try to show up as something ridicu-

lously vulgar and therefore unworthy of acceptance.

Such an attitude is typical of Gogol's writings and even of his style. For in contrast to Pushkin's dynamic and disciplined calm, the style of Gogol is agitated, emphatic, full of superlatives and always ready to pass from solemn, at times almost hypnotic exuberance, to a realistic accumulation of details, especially if these can be twisted and distorted into something grotesque. His ornate lyrical passages verge on rhetoric, the pitfalls of which he avoids only thanks to his uncanny sense of verbal rhythm and music. At the same time his realism of the *petits faits* and of the grimaces of life is unforgettable precisely on account of his rancorously comic exaggerations. All this makes Gogol one of the puzzling figures between the romantic and the realistic periods in literature—puzzling both as a writer and as a personality, since, in his case, it is impossible to separate the one from the other. This is why a few biographical data may be helpful in our approach.

II

BORN IN 1809 INTO AN IMPOVERISHED UKRAINIAN gentry family of Cossack stock, Gogol spent his childhood in the idyllic countryside near Poltava. From 1821 until 1828 he was educated at the Grammar School in Nyezhin and then lived, for some eight years, in Petersburg, which represented the greatest possible contrast to his warm and sunny Ukraine. The years between 1836 and 1849 he spent chiefly in Rome—always dear to his romantic temperament. In 1849 he returned to Russia and stayed for the most part in Moscow, where he died in February, 1852.

Small and not very prepossessing in appearance, Gogol was rather nervous by disposition. As though under the weight of a social and moral "inferiority complex," he became introspective and was always ready to attack in others the defects from which he himself suffered or thought he suffered. This fostered not only his gift of observation (confined to negative features only), but also that intensely satirical and ridiculing vein which became so conspicuous in his writings. At the same time he was anxious to counter, even as a schoolboy, the feeling of his inferiority by compensatory day-dreams of his future greatness. While still at Nyezhin, he indulged in visions of a brilliant career waiting for him, and it may have been with such hopes that, at the age of nineteen, he came to Petersburg. But it did not take long for a naïve provincial youth to discover that without money and connections he was less than a nobody in that cold and inhospitable city. Having tried his luck repeatedly but without success, he decided to flee to America. He took a boat to Lübeck, but as the little sum at his disposal was by then exhausted, he had to return and make new efforts to find a living. This time he obtained a humble underpaid post in one of the Government offices.

A victim of circumstance and disillusionment, Gogol

—like so many impoverished sons of the gentry—was in danger of becoming a failure, a social *déclassé*. But chance intervened, and the whole of his life underwent a sudden change. Having dabbled in literature while still a schoolboy, he now renewed his efforts in this direction chiefly as a means of escape from the dreary reality which preyed upon him. The tales he had once heard from his Cossack grandfather, the picturesque life and folk-lore of the people, the sun-drenched landscape of the south, the banks of the Dnieper, the expanse of the steppe—all this came back to his memory with an alluring halo and shaped itself into a number of stories, published (1831-32) in two volumes under the general title, *Evenings on a Farm near Dikanka*, which were an immediate success. Their appeal was enhanced by their folk-lore flavour, which happened to be the fashion of the day. In spite of certain touches of Tieck and of Hoffmann, Gogol's romanticism, as exemplified here, had all the flavour of the colourful Ukrainian countryside. The same holds good of Gogol's boisterous humour. The compositors setting the text were so amused by some of the pages that their laughter interfered with their work. Furthermore, the rhythm and the texture of Gogol's prose brought a new note into Russian fiction, which the readers were by no means slow to appreciate. While dexterously blending romantic themes with the spirit of the folk-lore, Gogol created an agitated and ornate style of his own. His pages were full of verbal embroideries as though he had wanted to lull himself into a trance by the music of his own language. The very first story, *The Fair of Sorochintsy* (turned by Borodin into an opera) opens with a description of a Ukrainian summer day, abounding in so many superlatives and metaphors that, but for its musical quality, it would resemble an oleographic improvisation. The moods and the motifs vary, and after situations full of boisterous fun and gaiety, one comes across such a story as *A Cruel Vengeance*, which is more gruesome than anything Edgar Allan Poe had ever imagined. Constructed in the spirit of a folk-ballad and told in a language redolent of poetry, it is full of a magic of its own, emanating from Gogol's own verbal rhythm and music.

In the whole collection there is only one story, *Ivan Shponka and his Aunty*, in which the realistic method prevails. But, significantly enough, Gogol left it unfinished, although here already he clearly shows that grotesque Hogarth-like quality which, in some of his later works, he developed to perfection. Otherwise the humour and the buffoonery of the *Evenings* abound in an over-loud gaiety which he probably intended to be both a refuge and a tonic. He himself said a few years later: "The cause of that gaiety which has been noticed in my first works was an inner need. I became a prey to fits of melancholy which were beyond my comprehension. . . . In order to get rid of them I invented the funniest things I could think of. I invented funny characters in the funniest situations imaginable."

But the word "invented" is perhaps not right, since Gogol's inventive fancy was much weaker than his imagination, and the latter was predominantly of an intensifying kind. Instead of inventing complicated plots of his own, he organised and intensified those he had heard from other people. And as for his realism, its propensity towards grotesque and satirical distortions is here not yet imbued with that *ressentiment* which became so conspicuous a feature in his works after *Evenings*. Externally, Gogol's "realistic" manner has quite a few features in common with that of Dickens, yet it would be wrong to compare the two in the way it is often done. For one thing, Dickens is devoid of Gogol's incurable rancour with regard to life ; so he can afford to be affirmative even when he ridicules. The "realism" of Gogol, on the other hand, is that of a frustrated romantic : like the negative realism of Gustave Flaubert or of Thomas Hardy. And this came out in his next collection of four narratives published under the title of *Mirgorod* (1835).

III

THESE STORIES, WHICH AT FIRST LOOK LIKE A continuation of *Evenings*, mark the dividing line between the romantic and the realistic manner in Gogol's art. Two of them, *Taras Bulba* and *Viy*, are romantic in the extreme, while the other two, *The Old-World Landowners* and *How the Two Ivans Quarrelled*, are—technically at least—as realistic as they can be. *Taras Bulba* is above all a romance of the Cossack past. Although inspired by the Waverley Novels, it is spun out in Gogol's ornate and agitated manner at its best. As in *A Cruel Vengeance*, here, too, the Cossack lore is turned into a gorgeous narrative reminiscent of ballad poetry. The old Cossack leader Taras, the executioner of his own son, who (prompted by his love for a Polish belle) had gone over to the enemy, might have been taken straight from a folk-ballad. Some other figures—the comic Jew Yankel and the swaggering Poles—have much in common with the *vertep* or the traditional Ukrainian puppet show for the people. The whole of it is told with unflagging verve, and some descriptive passages—the night in the steppe, for example, the riotous Cossack life in Syetch, the scenes of starvation in the beleaguered city, the battle episodes—are unforgettable. This work is often referred to, and rightly so, as the Cossack *Iliad*.

A strong romantic flavour of the same creepy variety as in *A Cruel Vengeance* emanates from the story *Viy*. According to Gogol's so far unverified assertion, Viy is the name of a symbolic monster taken from the Ukrainian folk-lore. But the nightmare-like monster as represented here is the projection of certain disturbing fears and phobias, stored up in Gogol's own "racial" unconscious. It is as complex a story as the two realistic narratives, included in the volume, are simple in their subject-matter. In *The Old-World Landowners* there is hardly a plot at all. The whole of it is a genre picture (in the Dutch manner) describing the vegetative existence of an aged couple: a kind of Ukrainian Darby and Joan, whose thoughts never go beyond the fence of their orchard. The principal function of their idyllic life is eating and sleeping, yet both of them are contented and so touchingly attached to each other that when old Pulcheria suddenly dies, her husband is past consolation and follows her soon after. It seems as though Gogol had put into this story his own sentimental-romantic nostalgia for a haven of peace, even vegetative peace, amidst the turmoil of his metropolitan experiences.

The same kind of vegetative existence permeates the opening chapter of *How the Two Ivans Quarrelled*,* but this time from a different angle. Nostalgia is here replaced by invective. The plot is again slender, but even such as it is, Gogol borrowed it from another Ukrainian—the older writer Narezhny. The story depicts two bosom friends who for some utterly idiotic reason quarrelled and started a series of litigations, dragging them on and on until both of them were ruined. Here, for the first time, Gogol's comic laughter turned into that proverbial "laughter through tears" which, from now on, clung to him with an increasingly sinister ring. His realism à la Hogarth made him depict the negative features of his characters, as well as of life in general, with all the indignation of a wounded romantic. Gloom and sadness which lurk behind this otherwise comic story, protrude quite plainly towards the end, this description of the author's departure from Mirgorod providing the final touch: "The lean nags famous in Mirgorod as post-horses began to stamp their hoofs, which were buried

* The Russian title is *A Story of the Quarrel Between Ivan Ivanovich and Ivan Nikifirovich.*

in a grey mass of mud, with a sound displeasing to the ear. The rain poured in torrents upon the Jew seated in the box, covered with a rug. The dampness penetrated to my very bones. The dreary barrier with a sentry-box in which an old soldier sat repairing his weapons, was passed slowly by. Once again the same fields, black in the places where they had been dug up, and of a greenish hue in others ; wet daws and crows ; monotonous rain, a tearful sky, without one gleam of light ! . . . A gloomy place—this world, gentlemen !"

IV

"A GLOOMY PLACE—THIS WORLD, GENTLEMEN," became from now on Gogol's motto as well as his basic disposition. But he masked it by his laughter in which he found first an escape from life and then a means for revenge upon life. Unable to escape from reality, he tried to fight it by laughing at its ugliness and drabness, which he did with all the vindictiveness at his disposal. It was here that Gogol's romantic temperament often took on a highly realistic garb, notably from his Petersburg stories onwards. Three of these, *A Portrait*, *The Nevsky Prospect* and *The Diary of a Madman*, appeared in his miscellany, *Arabesques* (1835). *The Nose* was written about the same period, and his famous *Greatcoat* some four or five years later.

The least satisfactory from an artistic standpoint is *A Portrait*. Its romanticism may remind one of Hoffmann's *Die Elexiere des Teufels*, or of Maturin's *Melmoth the Wanderer* (which Gogol read in a Russian translation). On the other hand, the story contains some of Gogol's own dilemmas and inhibitions, one of them being his belief in the demoniacal agencies inherent in life itself. We find in it also his conception of art as the promoter of moral good. Similarly revealing is *The Nevsky Prospect*, which expresses Gogol's wounded idealism perhaps more directly than any other narrative of his.

Apart from his "romantic irony," Gogol introduced here the background of the big city in its negative and de-humanising aspects. These came out even more potently in *The Diary of a Madman* and *The Greatcoat*, depicting the two varieties of one and the same "little man:" the humble office drudge, victimised by the big city—a predicament that (but for a lucky chance) might well have been in store for Gogol himself. While working in the Government office, he was able to study this type from personal observations. Hence the detailed concreteness of his portrayals.

However insignificant in life, Poprishchin—the hero of *The Diary of a Madman*—does not entirely surrender to his fate, but entrenches himself behind all sorts of wishful thinking and day-dreams, the object of which is the daughter of his omnipotent chief. He is in love with her, although the pretty girl does not even condescend to be aware of him. This plunges him all the more deeply into his compensatory dream-world, duly recorded in his diary. The heavier the blows he has to endure, the stronger is his self-concocted antidote.

And when he learns at last that his idol has become betrothed to one of those "social betters" whose hollow glitter is despised—in his opinion—by the very dogs, his imaginary grandeur takes on the size of his defeat: he is no longer a nonentity, an underpaid scribe, but His Majesty Ferdinand VIII, the fugitive King of Spain. His manners assume at once a style in keeping with such an exalted position. Even when he is taken to the lunatic asylum, he sees and interprets everything only in this light. During the painful manipulations he is here compelled to undergo, a momentary idea as to his condition flashes through his mind, but the world of madness closes upon him once again and for good.

Akaky, the hero of *The Greatcoat*, is another Poprishchin, but—this time—aged and battered enough to accept his humble place in life without grumbling. The highest ambition he can still rise to is to scrape together enough money to buy a fashionable greatcoat—with marten collar and all. With great difficulties he makes his dream come true, and one morning he appears in the office in a smart greatcoat—like a real somebody. General surprise is crowned by his being invited to an evening party, at which he drinks too much and leaves the company rather late at night. While crossing a lonely square, he is knocked down by two individuals and, when he comes to himself, there is no trace left either of the thieves or of his greatcoat. Full of despair Akaky falls ill and dies of grief. Such is the gist of this masterpiece of *Kleinmalerei*, which exercised a strong influence on the development of Russian realism.

Gogol's remaining Petersburg story, *The Nose*, can best be described as a fantasy constructed on the pattern of a dream—something like *Alice in Wonderland*, but probably suggested by the "nosological" passages in *Tristram Shandy* (he knew it from a Russian translation). Devoid of any surface logic, it is yet—like *A Cruel Vengeance* and *Viy*—of great value to anyone interested in the workings of the subconscious mind, and especially in the meeting point between psycho-analysis and literature. Its amusingly grotesque jumble hides what has been called Gogol's castration-complex, as well as a few other peculiarities of his sexual life. In this respect it is connected with certain passages of Poprishchin's gibberish in *The Diary of a Madman*, notably with those describing the earth falling upon the moon.

V

FURTHER ASPECTS OF GOGOL'S ART CAN BE GLEANED FROM his satirical comedy, *The Government Inspector* (1836), and his novel *Dead Souls* (1842), both of which occupy a very high place in Russian literature. The plots even for these two works were not invented by Gogol—they were suggested to him by Pushkin ; yet Gogol worked them out into masterpieces in which, amongst other things, he gave full scope to his "laughter through tears." With *The Government Inspector*, Gogol's laughter assumed, moreover, a deliberately castigating and moral role. He himself acknowledged later in his *An Author's Confession*: "I saw that in my former works I laughed in vain, uselessly, without knowing why. But if we must laugh, why not laugh at what really deserves to be laughed at by us all. In my *Government Inspector* I decided to bring together and to deride all that is bad in Russia, all the evils which are being perpetrated in those places where utmost rectitude is required from man."

Here Gogol's attention was focused on the corrupt bureaucracy, and with so much malice, too, that this comedy rightly belongs to the most biting specimens of its kind. The plot is simple. An irresponsible windbag, Khlestakov by name, who, together with his servant, travels from St. Petersburg to his father's village, loses at cards in a god-forsaken provincial town all his money and is in danger of being put into jail for his inability to pay the hotel bill. The *gorodnichy* (police governor) of the town expects at that time the incognito arrival of a Government Inspector, the very thought of whom makes him shudder. Nor are the other officials in an elated state of mind, and they know why. Two of the local worthies, who have just seen in the restaurant the starved Khlestakov rather wistfully inspecting other people's meals, come upon the idea that the inquisitive, smartly dressed stranger is most likely the dreaded incognito. Unanimously, the officials decide to bribe him, and the *gorodnichy*—an expert in these matters—goes personally to the hotel. Frightened at first by the visit and then puzzled by it, Khlestakov soon regains his aplomb and enters into his new role with relish. He is fêted, bribed, shown the institutions of the town, and even becomes betrothed to the *gorodnichy's* daughter. Fortunately, Khlestakov's sagacious servant guesses that the worthy gentlemen must have taken his master for someone of consequence and urges him to leave the hospitable town before it is too late. So the would-be inspector departs—his head full of pleasant memories and his pockets bulging with money. In order to reassure all the nice folk around him, he promises, of course, to be back in time for the wedding. The *gorodnichy's* arrogance is now unbounded. Puffed up by the dreams of his future greatness under the wing of such a mighty son-in-law, he bullies the town people more than ever. All the townsmen of any importance are so anxious to ingratiate themselves in turn that they hurry at once, together with their spouses, to congratulate him. It is a grand and animated gathering. But suddenly, like a thunderbolt from the blue, the truth leaks out that the Government Inspector was an impostor. The local postmaster, always willing to increase his knowledge by reading other people's letters, could not resist opening the one Khlestakov had written to a pal in Petersburg, boasting in the frankest terms possible of all that had befallen him in that blessed town. As the postmaster has brought the letter to the gathering, its effect can be imagined. But when the general consternation is at its height, a gendarme enters with the announcement that the real Government Inspector has just arrived and demands an immediate interview with the *gorodnichy*. Here the curtain slowly falls.

N I K O L A I   G O G O L

The Government Inspector is a condensed picture of all the rottenness, corruption and stupidity of that bureaucratic Russia which Gogol knew so well. The portraiture is, once more, thoroughly Hogarthian. As a satirical comedy of manners, the play actually continued the tradition which had started with the eighteenth-century playwright Fonvizin, and reached something of a climax in Griboyedov's *Woe from Wit* (1823). Its effect was bound to be overwhelming in the "leaden" atmosphere of the Nicholas regime. The first performance, on 19th March, 1836, took place by a special order of the Tsar himself who, this time, overruled the official censorship and came personally to see the production. "Everyone has received his due, and I most of all," Nicholas I is reported to have said after the performance.* But the gall contained in the comedy was too much for those concerned. A hue and cry was raised against Gogol and before long assumed such proportions that he preferred to leave Russia altogether. He settled down in Rome where he remained, with various interruptions, until 1848. It was in Rome, too, that he completed his greatest work, *Dead Souls*.

* Space does not permit us to discuss Gogol's other plays. Suffice it to say that, apart from some dramatic fragments, two more plays stand to his credit: *Marriage* and *Gamblers*. The first deals with the conservative merchants milieu which, after Gogol, was so successfully taken up by A. Ostrovsky, the greatest playwright of the realistic period in Russia. The second is based on the theme of cheating the cheat and is powerful in its cleverly-worked-out denouement.

NIKOLAI GOGOL

VI

THIS NOVEL, WHICH BY NOW HAS ACHIEVED ITS RIGHTFUL place in the literature of the world, is difficult to classify. Gogol himself called it an epic (*poema*). Like some of his other works, it is devoid of an involved plot and even the love motif, so essential in a novel, is here absent. The chapters follow one another like those of an old-fashioned picaresque narrative, the episodes of which are connected by the central character only—a rogue, a travelling adventurer, or both. The book should really be called *Dead Serfs* ; but as serfs were nicknamed "souls" in Russia, its title has a businesslike and a symbolic meaning in one. Chichikov, the hero of the novel, is a travelling businessman and a swindler, but with the stamp of an immaculate gentleman. The aim of his journey is to buy up a number of those serfs who have died so recently that they have not yet been struck off the register and are therefore officially recorded as being still alive. "Now it is good time," he reasons, "there has just been an epidemic, the peasants have died, thank goodness, in great numbers." Chichikov's intention is to mortgage such fictitious serfs in a bank for a substantial sum of money, after which he would disappear and start a respectable existence in some province sufficiently remote to hide his past. This would not be too difficult, since his manners and appearance are so winning that everybody is charmed by him. In the district town, chosen by him as the starting point for his errands, he is simply worshipped, at least during the first few days of his stay. But he has no time for adulation. He means business, and so a visiting tour to those landowners in the district who might be of use to him, cannot be delayed.

His interviews introduce to the reader a number of magnificent portraits in Gogol's style at its best. Their characteristics are brought out so intensely that they often verge on grotesque spooks, while yet remaining concrete and real. Manilov; Sobakevich* ; the miser Plyushkin ; the professional cheat and scandalmonger Nozdryov—they all parade before us like so many caricatures of humanity, seen with the eyes of a Hogarth or a Breughel. What increases the comicality of Chichikov himself is the contrast between the gentlemanliness of his appearance on the one hand, and the criminal nature of his errand on the other. Realising the delicate task he is engaged in, he broaches the subject with due circumspection, but his manoeuvres invariably lead up to the question whether and how many dead "souls" are available—a kind of groping which, apart from its comic touches, is bound to give away the moral level of both Chichikov and his interlocutor. In the end Chichikov's eagerness to get rich quickly outstrips even his caution : he blurts out a word too much where silence would be wisdom. As a result the news about his strange purchases leaks out, and the same town which at first welcomed him as a paragon of personal and social charm, is all at once

* From the Russian word *sobaka,* the dog. Like Dickens, Gogol was a master at inventing suggestive names, most of which are untranslatable.

astir with the wildest rumours about his doings and even about his identity. Sensible enough to clear out, Chichikov makes a hasty departure in his *troika* (a coach drawn by three horses) at the end of the first volume—the only one that was finished. Yet quite unexpectedly, the concluding note of this volume is a personal lyrical digression on the part of Gogol himself. In contrast to the general mood of the work, the ending strikes (in a major key and in a manner which can serve as an example of Gogol's temperamental style) a regular paean to the *troika* and the wide open spaces of Russia. In the same passage, Gogol addresses Russia with a question which all her great authors have been asking since—asking in vain. But here is the passage itself:

"Chichikov was fond of fast driving, and as he rocked on the leather cushion he only smiled at the bumps. And what Russian does not love fast driving ? And how should his soul not love it ? For is he not prone to surrender to the sudden whirl of a spree ? Is he not liable to cast discretion to the winds, saying 'the devil take it all' ? And therefore is not fast driving his delight ? How can he not love its magic and incantation ? And is not a galloping troika like a mysterious force that has swept you away on its wings, so that you find yourself flying along, and everything else is flying with you ? The milestones fly past to meet you, the merchants in their carts are flying by, on each side of you forests of dark fir and pine-trees are flying past to the thump of axes and the croaking of crows, the whole of the highway is flying on, no one knows where, into the receding distance ; and there is a lurking terror in that glimmer of objects that keep flashing by rapidly and are gone before they can be identified ; and only the sky overhead, the nimble clouds, and the emergent moon, appear motionless. Ah, you troika ! Bird-like troika, who invented you ? Surely you could only have been born among a spirited people—in a land which does not stop at jokes but has taken half the world in the embrace of its smooth plains so that one can go and count the milestones till one's head turns dizzy ! Nor does it seem that much cunning was required to fabricate a sledge or carriage drawn by those three horses ; it was improvised with the help of an axe and a drill by some handy Yaroslavl peasant. Your driver wears no great top boots of foreign make: he is all beard and mittens, and sits perched on his seat the devil knows how ; but when he stands up, cracks his whip and starts up a song, then the horses rush like a hurricane, the spokes of the wheels spin in one smooth disk, and only the road shudders beneath them while some passer-by cries out as he stops in alarm ! And the troika is off and away, away ! . . . And very soon there is only a swirl of dust on the horizon.

"Russia, are you not speeding along like a fiery and matchless troika ? Beneath you the road is smoke, the bridges thunder, and everything is left far behind. At your passage the onlooker stops amazed as by a miracle divine. 'Was that not a flash of lightning ?' he asks. What is this surge so full of terror ? And what is this force unknown impelling these horses never seen before? Ah, you horses, horses,—what horses! Your manes are whirlwind! And are your veins not tingling like a quick ear? Descending from above you have caught the note of the familiar song; and at once, in unison, you strain your chests of bronze and, with your hooves barely skimming the earth, you are transformed into arrows, into straight lines winging through the air, and on you rush under divine inspiration! . . . Russia, where are you flying? Answer me. There is no answer. The bells are tinkling and filling the air with their wonderful pealing: the air is rent and thundering as it turns to wind; everything on earth comes flying past and, looking askance at her, other peoples and States move aside and make way."*

VII

IT IS HARDLY NECESSARY TO EXPLAIN THE SYMBOLIC meaning of the lines quoted. The enigma of the same endless irrational Russia crops up similarly in a number of authors, including Alexander Blok—the greatest symbolist poet modern Russia has produced. But as for Gogol's novel, even such a spirited finale does not make up for the unpleasant pictures spread over the rest of the book. Their sharp outlines remain in the reader's

* Translated by George Reavey, in the Novel Library (Hamish Hamilton).

mind for good. They may not contain any direct propaganda against the serfdom system as such, yet indirectly they did a great deal to draw attention to the anomaly of its existence. Gogol himself was interested also in some other issues to which he gave vent in this masterpiece. If in *The Government Inspector* he dealt a blow at the bureaucratic regime of Nicholas I, in *Dead Souls* he attacked the vulgarity of life as a whole. The hidden romantic in Gogol now took revenge for his frustrations by laughing at life more maliciously than in any of his previous works. And the method he made use of was again that of realistic *Kleinmalerei*. He once complained that the critics who "dissected my literary talent were not able to find the essential traits of my nature. Pushkin alone was able to see them. He used to say that no other writer was endowed with my capacity for bringing out all the trivialities of life and for opening one's eyes on those trifles, which, as a rule, remain unnoticed."

Vulgarity and drabness, presented in *Dead Souls*, are thus symbolic in the very intensity of their realism which seems to imply that something must be wrong with the transcendental inner core of life, or of what Gogol understood by life.

Vulgarity as something immanent in existence became in fact Gogol's *idée fixe* which he added to his habitual moral hypochondria. Conscious of his own defects, he was the more aware of all that was negative and nasty in the world with which he could never come to terms. Hence his restlessness of a man who is impelled to be eternally on the move, as though vainly trying to escape from reality and from himself. After 1836 he lived mostly in Italy, but travelled also in France, Switzerland, Germany, feeling everywhere an uprooted stranger and a prey to his own ennui. "Before the eyes of all there only grows the gigantic figure of Tedium," he wrote in 1847. "It grows and assumes infinite dimensions day in, day out. O Lord! Empty and terrible is Thy world!"

Gogol's aggressive realism became directed above all against this Tedium—outside and even more within himself. His fight with the defects in the world around was in essence a fight with himself. "While attacking some bad trait of mine," he says, "I presented it in a different rôle and tried to make it appear in my own eyes as a deadly fiend who has injured me terribly. Then I persecuted it with malice and irony, with anything I could. But had anyone seen those monsters which came from under my pen in my first drafts, he would have shivered with fear." The subjective root of his realism is thus obvious. On the other hand, once art has become a weapon of this kind, then a much too conscious moral purpose or even moral mission, bestowed as it were by God Himself, is likely to be one of its dangerous temptations. This was what happened to Gogol's art after he had witnessed the chastising moral effect of *The Government Inspector* and *Dead Souls*. In order to be worthy of his high mission in spite of his "sins," he did all he could to deserve God's grace by rigorous ascetic practices—like the ones described in the second part of *The Portrait*. Unfortunately, this mood coincided with a period when his artistic inspiration was at an ebb. So he increased his didactic propensity and began to talk as one having authority even concerning things he knew little or nothing about. At a time when the Russian intelligentsia, led by Belinsky, was fighting for a more liberal and progressive system of life, the incurably romantic Gogol continued to look upon such institutions as State, Church, serfdom, autocracy and education in a bigoted conservative and patriarchal spirit. To make things worse, he decided to enlighten his readers upon these matters. In the hope that the whole of Russia would listen to his "Christian" sermons with the same enthusiasm as she had hitherto welcomed his literary works, he published (in 1847) his *Selected Passages from Correspondence with My Friends*.

This book was responsible for the most painful shock in Gogol's life. Instead of resounding all over Russia like a prophet, he was overwhelmed with attacks, criticism and derision which came not only from the radical-minded intellectuals but even from some of his own friends in the conservative Slavophil camp. The most slashing blow came, however, from his former admirer Belinsky, who in a letter—now famous—called Gogol a preacher of the knout, an apostle of ignorance, a defender of obscurantism and darkest oppression. "You are only bemused and not enlightened, you have understood neither the form nor the spirit of contemporary Christianity. It is not the truth of Christian teaching that your book breathes, but the fear of death, of the devil, and of hell." Which was largely but not entirely true. In spite of that, the violent attacks on *Selected Passages* helped to raise and partly to clear certain problems in the light of which Gogol's own position grew worse and more ridiculous. Unable to parry the blows, he wrote—in July 1847—to his friend Sergey Aksakov (the author of *A Family Chronicle*): "Impatience made me publish my book. Seeing that I would not be able to master my *Dead Souls*, and genuinely grieving over the colourlessness of modern literature which indulges in empty discussions, I hurried to say a word or two on the problems I was interested in; the problems which I had wanted to develop or else to embody in living images and characters." And this brings us again to his *Dead Souls*.

Gogol had the serious intention of following up the success of the first volume of this novel by another two volumes, and turning the whole of it into a kind of *Divina Commedia* of Russian life—with an important "message" attached to it. The first part, presenting only the negative side of Russian life, was to be its *Inferno*. The second part was planned, like Dante's *Purgatory*, on a higher level, while the third would deal with Chichikov's moral rebirth. But such a task required convincing portraits of positive characters, and these were beyond Gogol's power, since his sources of inspiration were confined to indictment and laughter. Thus in the remaining five chapters of the second volume of *Dead Souls* (on which he laboured for eleven years) the virtuous characters look artificial and stilted, whereas the negative ones are portrayed with vigour, although one cannot help noticing that Gogol's former verve was cooling down—a process by which the author himself was seriously perturbed.

VIII

GOGOL ACKNOWLEGED IN HIS LETTER TO AKSAKOV that he had hastened to publish *Selected Passages from Correspondence* partly because he felt he was unable to cope with the creative task imposed upon him by *Dead Souls*, and therefore wanted to give Russia at least the benefit of his message. Gogol the Teacher, severed from his art, had however little to say, and what he did say was neither new nor particularly interesting. The very fact that he published it in such a shape was a proof that he was beginning to doubt his former artistic power. And since he regarded—quite in the spirit of romanticism—his literary genius as a special gift from on high, he was bound to interpret the drying up of his artistic inspiration as being tantamount to a withdrawal of God's grace in punishment for his "sins." Morbidly conscious of certain weaknesses which were partly due to his underdeveloped sex, he considered himself a great sinner. He repented, prayed, mortified his flesh, and even undertook a pilgrimage to Palestine, but it was all to no purpose. Neither the glow of literary creation nor that of religious fervour was now granted to him. What Gogol called his religious feeling was mostly composed of the atavistic fear of the devil and hell Belinsky had alluded to. Gogol himself wrote in a letter before his departure to Palestine (12th February 1848) as follows: "It even seems to me I have no religion. I confess Christ only because my reason commands me to. I only have the will to believe and, in spite of this, I still dare to go on a pilgrimage to our Saviour's tomb. Oh, do pray for me!"

The cry, "Oh, do pray for me!" became even more frequent after his journey to Jerusalem which had left him inwardly as cold, frightened and bewildered as ever. His state of mind was aggravated by forebodings of imminent death. Was he ready for it? What answer would he give to the inexorable Judge? While in the throes of such moods and torments, he fell under the spell of an ignorant despotic priest, Father Konstantinovsky, who, playing on Gogol's fears, bullied him into spiritual submission. It was probably due to him that on the night of 11th February 1852, Gogol burned the completed MS. of the second volume of *Dead Souls*.

In that night he prayed with great contrition, after which he called his boy-servant and wandered through the rooms, in each of them making a sign of the cross. Finally, he took out of the portfolio his MS. (the second volume of *Dead Souls*), threw it into the fireplace and lit it with the candle. The boy protested, but Gogol's only answer was, "This is not your business—you must pray." When the sheets were burned, he crossed himself, kissed the boy, shuffled to his bedroom, fell upon the divan and began to cry. A few days later, on 21st February, he died—probably from physical exhaustion due to his ascetic practices.

IX

LESS STUDIED ABROAD THAN SOME OTHER RUSSIAN authors, Gogol yet occupies one of the most important places in the fiction of his country. It was the heritage of Pushkin and of Gogol that determined the character as well as the trend of modern Russian literature. Whereas the Apollonian genius of Pushkin bequeathed to it its lucidity, simplicity and plastic power, Gogol was responsible for its disturbing subjectivism, inner quest and vexation of the spirit, in which he anticipated both Dostoevsky and Tolstoy. He, moreover, laid stress on the portraiture of characters at the expense of a well-constructed plot and (following Pushkin) sanctioned the "little man" as a subject worthy of literary treatment—the two features which were adopted by the majority of subsequent Russian authors. The "natural school," championed by Belinsky, took from Gogol above all the realism of "small facts" and also that humanitarian note of pity which was stressed in Gogol's *Greatcoat* and assumed, later on, such gigantic proportions in Dostoevsky's works. "We have all come from under Gogol's *Greatcoat*," Dostoevsky said of the writers of his generation at a time when the monumental Russian realism was already at its height.

Akaky certainly had a long literary progeny of the "insulted and the injured," beginning with Dostoevsky's own *Poor Folk* (1846). Even Dostoevsky's "pathological" trend, from his story *The Double* onwards, has one of its sources in *The Diary of a Madman.* Gogol's Petersburg stories, on the other hand, introduced (together with Pushkin's *Queen of Spades* and *The Bronze Horseman*), that "irrational" atmosphere of the Tsarist metropolis which was expanded and deepened by Dostoevsky and, at the beginning of this century, by Andrey Bely.

What affected, however, a large number of Russian writers was not Gogol's style, but his peculiar attitude towards life and the world. His realism of a frustrated (and therefore rancorous) romantic idealist is conspicuous in the work of such authors as Pisemsky and Saltykov-Shchedrin. As for the other elements of his writings, Goncharov took on and continued Gogol's realism of the minute *petits faits.* In addition, the two principal characters (Oblomov and Stolz) in Goncharov's great novel *Oblomov*, are obviously a further elaboration of Tentetnikov and Konstănzhoglo in the second volume of *Dead Souls.* Gogol's agitated prose was carried on mainly by Dostoevsky. Its rhythmical and ornate character was investigated and further developed by the modernist Andrey Bely, who, together with Alexey Remizov, was responsible for some of the most interesting recent experiments upon the Russian prose style.

Last but not least, it was in Gogol's works and in his "laughter through tears" that literature made a decided attempt to become also a moral and social force in life—a tendency which was fully endorsed by the authors who came after him : from Nekrasov to Tolstoy, and from Saltykov-Shchedrin to Gorky. In our days it is being endorsed, whether for better or for worse, by the representatives of socialist realism in the Soviet Union. All that is vital in Gogol's work thus remains an inalienable part of the literary heritage in Russia, no matter what changes may take place in her politics, in her taste, or in her general outlook upon life and the world.

THREE

Lermontov

I

THE ROMANTIC MOVEMENT, FOR VARIOUS REASONS, affected Russia less many-sidedly than was the case with other European countries. The influence of Byronism itself was limited to some of its aspects, and even those were partly conditioned by a regime under the pressure of which the few liberties of the country seemed to be going from bad to worse. In Pushkin's day there was at least the atmosphere of the *pléiade*, the members of which firmly believed in literary culture and were able to stimulate one another. The growing vigilance of the Nicholas regime made a collaboration on such a scale impossible even in matters of culture, let alone politics. As there was no outlet for any independent initiative and ambition of one's own, a number of gifted young men were bound to turn into "superfluous" Childe Harolds of the peculiar Russian brand, so conspicuous in the literature of that country. But the danger of maladjustment loomed large from another quarter also. There were signs that the patriarchal-feudal system, based on serfdom, would have to yield, before long, to the advent of a capitalist era, demanding an economic as well as psychological change which could not be achieved overnight. A feeling of uncertainty, vacillation and general uprootedness was in the air, and no gendarmes, no political straitjackets were able to eliminate the bewilderment arising in men's minds.

In this respect, too, there was a difference between the generation of Pushkin and that to which his immediate successor, the poet Mikhail Lermontov, belonged. In spite of all personal adversities, Pushkin was still rooted in his age, in his class and in the culture of which the members of the advanced gentry-elite were rightly proud. Even the "Decembrists" who rebelled in 1825, did so because they believed in certain values which they, as the most progressive representatives of their own class, were called upon to uphold. Yet the social and mental atmosphere in the next generation was no longer the same. The leadership on the part of a gentry-elite became impossible, because such an elite as a compact group or body no longer existed. The best representatives of that class suddenly found themselves in a vacuum. Even the slowly emerging intelligentsia—an amalgam of the gentry intellectuals and the educated "commoners"—was of no use to many of those who were unable or else unwilling to adapt themselves to the spirit of the age. And Lermontov, for all his genius, was the least adaptable of men.

This fact alone determined the basic character of his work. If Pushkin introduced the "superfluous man" on a romantic or quasi-romantic plane, Lermontov added two salient features to this phenomenon. First, he deepened the *inner* isolation of such an uprooted individual until he touched upon that metaphysical region which, later on, was so disturbingly tackled by Dostoevsky. And secondly, he gave a psychological analysis of a tragic Russian descendant of Childe Harold (via Pushkin's Onegin) so brilliantly as to affect thereby, romantic though he was, quite a few facets of Russian realism. He is still regarded as being the greatest and also the most Byronic romanticist in Russian literature ; yet his Byronism was not an imitation but had certain definite traits of its own. He himself said in one of his early poems :

No, I'm not Byron, I'm different,
I'm still unknown, a man apart,
Like Byron by the world rejected,
*Only I have a Russian heart.**

In spite of this "Russian heart" on which he insists, or perhaps because of it, Lermontov's *mal du siècle*, with all its romantic ingredients, sprang not only from social but also from what might be termed spiritual causes. His nostalgia resembled that of a fallen denizen of a different timeless realm, who still vaguely remembers its enchantment and therefore finds it impossible to fit into any conditions of the actual world, least of all into those of Russia under Nicholas I.

* This and the next poem are translated by V. de Sola Pinto.

LERMONTOV

When Lermontov was only seventeen, he wrote the following poem, called *The Angel*, which may provide a clue to the undercurrents of his romanticism:

An angel was flying through night's deep blue
And softly he sang as he flew.
Moon, stars and clouds in a wondering throng
Listened rapt by that heavenly song.

He sang of the blest, who live without stain
In God's garden, a shining train.
He hymned the Lord's might, and his voice rang clear,
For he sang without guile and fear.

He bore in his arms a young soul to its birth
On the dark and sinful earth,
And the Angel's song remained in the soul
Without words yet unblemished and whole.

Long after on earth when the soul would tire,
It felt a strange, aching desire
For the music of heaven which it sought for in vain
In earth's songs of sorrow and pain.

The poem could serve as an epigraph to the whole of Lermontov's work. It goes a long way to explain his difference from Byron, the character of his pessimism, and of his protest against the realities he saw around. This again was intertwined with a number of less "transcendental" elements, the nature of which becomes clearer if we approach Lermontov through some of his biographic data. For in contrast to Pushkin, Lermontov was the first great poet in Russian literature who deliberately turned his entire work into an inner biography; into a direct or indirect personal confession of a poignant and often glowingly passionate kind.

II

BORN IN 1814, LERMONTOV HAD SOME SCOTTISH BLOOD in his veins. One of the Learmonths entered the Russian service at the beginning of the 17th century, settled in his adopted country and altered his ancestral name to make it sound Russian. (In some of his early poems, especially in *The Wish*, Lermontov alludes to Scotland as his distant homeland.) His father was an impoverished landowner who had married the daughter of a rich, capricious and overbearing woman and was always treated by his mother-in-law, Mme Arsenyeva, as a "poor relation." As his wife died after a few years of marriage, Mme Arsenyeva took her little grandson to her own estate where he was brought up until the age of twelve. Puzzled by the family quarrels, spoilt by his grandmother's adulation, and at the same time deprived of congenial companions, the boy must have felt lonely even in those formative years. Gradually he developed into a self-centred dreamer, anxious to conceal his passionate nature under the mask of aloofness, and his innate idealism behind the pose of callous flippancy. His poetic gift, which remained his only outlet for self-expression, began to develop rather early and was fostered by two circumstances: his visit to the Caucasus at the age of eleven, and his education in a Moscow boarding school (from 1827 onwards) which was not devoid of literary interests. Under the guidance of such teachers as Merzlyakov and Raitch, young Lermontov was initiated into the principal works of Russian literature, as well as into those of Byron, Moore, Goethe, Schiller and Scott. He was much impressed by Thomas Moore's biography of Byron (he read it in 1830) and, in his early years, his own translations from Byron helped him to work himself into Byronic moods. At the same time he cultivated his aloofness to such a degree that even on entering, in 1830, Moscow University, he showed but little inclination to mix with his fellow-students and paid hardly any attention to the fact that after the *débâcle* of the "Decembrists" the University of Moscow, with its debating circles, became the actual focus of Russian culture. The Stankevich circle, with the budding critic—the "commoner" Belinsky as one of its members—was exploring all sorts of literary and philosophic problems. The youths gathering round Herzen and the poet Ogaryov showed, however, a keener interest in the social questions of the day, the liberal "Decembrist" spirit still hovering over their debates.

Lermontov did not belong to any of these groups. Besides, in 1832 he suddenly left the University and went to Petersburg where he entered a military school and, after two years of detestable training, obtained a commission in the Guards. In 1837 he was transferred (or, rather, exiled) to a Caucasian regiment on account of his aggressive invective, *The Death of a Poet*, written on the day of Pushkin's death (January 29th). The poem could not be printed,* but as it was read in countless written copies, it made Lermontov's name known from one end of Russia to the other. In the Caucasus, which was fated to be strangely connected with his life, his work, and even with his death, he met another poet, the banished "Decembrist" Alexander Odoevsky—one of the few people he really befriended. Owing to his grandmother's influence, Lermontov was allowed to return at the end of the same year to his old Hussar regiment at St. Petersburg. By this time he was already regarded as one of the great hopes of Russian poetry and a successor of Pushkin. He was admired, lionised, but in spite of his numerous conquests among the society ladies, he remained as bored and lonely as ever. Mixing a life of dissipation with intensive poetic activities, he did not care to make himself popular either in society or among his own comrades. As for literary men, he knew very few and seemed to avoid them on purpose. After a duel he had in February 1840 with the son of the French ambassador, M. de Barrante, he was arrested and again sent to the Caucasus. He took part in some dangerous expeditions against the mountaineers, in which he displayed reckless courage. One of such engagements—the

* It first appeared in print in 1856, in Herzen's *Polar Star*, published in London. Two years later the poem was printed also in Russia.

battle on the river Valerik (on July 11th, 1840)—he described in a most beautiful poem. In spring 1841 he made a flying visit to Petersburg in the hope of being allowed to remain there, but without success. On his return to the Caucasus he stopped for a longer period at his favourite spa Pyatigorsk. The place was full of summer guests. Among them there were the ubiquitous "fashionable" people, including some of his old acquaintances. One of them, a certain Major Martynov, whom he tactlessly ridiculed in the presence of a lady, challenged him to a duel. The duel took place outside Pyatigorsk on July 27th, 1841, and the poet was killed on the spot. He died at the age of twenty-seven, i.e. ten years younger than Pushkin.

III

IN SPITE OF THIS, THE BEST OF LERMONTOV'S WORK IS second only to Pushkin's, but with reservations. Pushkin showed even in his early verse great technical skill and finish. In the case of Lermontov, however, it is only the mature work—roughly from 1836 onwards—that really counts. His youthful work compares with his later products chiefly as a series of experiments. He was perfectly aware of this and even kept returning to some of his themes again and again in order to perfect them during his later and more mature phases, until they received an adequate form. Yet however much he differed from Pushkin in his outlook and temperament, he could not do without Pushkin's influence. Even Byron was at first approached by him mainly through Pushkin. His two immature tales in verse, *The Circassian* and *The Prisoner of the Caucasus* (both written at the age of fifteen) were imitations of Pushkin's Byronic tales with the Caucasus as the exotic "Eastern" background. After a more thorough acquaintance with Byron's work Lermontov wrote his longer Caucasian tales *Ismail Bey* (1832) and *Hadji Abrek*, the latter having been his first longer poem to be printed in a periodical in 1835.

In the meantime Lermontov tried his hand also at plays. They are pretentiously romantic, redolent of Schiller's "storm and stress" period but much more juvenile and with an obvious tendency towards self-dramatisation. *Men and Passions* (to which, for some reason, he gave a German title, *Menschen und Leidenschaften*, 1830) and *A Queer Fellow* (1831) must have been written under the impact of the family quarrels between his grandmother and his father. His later drama, *The Masquerade* (1835), over-stated though it be, is more impressive in its combination of blind jealousy (the influence of *Othello*) on the one hand, and of a conflict between the self-centred individual and society on the other. Whereas Pushkin the poet could and did rise to that affirmative attitude which made him look sympathetically upon life at large, Lermontov was too often inclined to reduce the whole of life to the moods and demands of his own frustrated ego and to treat it accordingly. He also preferred to Pushkin's lucidly visual imagery the more visionary symbols often originating in the realm of the spirit (like his *Angel*), and the language of many an early poem of his seems rather blurred. At his best, however, he soon developed a matchless pictorial gift. Lermontov the romantic has certain features in common with the other-worldly romanticism of Zhukovsky ; yet instead of sharing Zhukovsky's passivity and quietism, he remained a "Byronic" rebel to the end. Like Byron, too, he broke morally with his own class, even if he was unable to do so socially. And as in the case of Byron again (or for that matter of Gogol), the virulence of his romantic indictment taught him to watch and to expose life also by realistic methods. These he kept perfecting with such success as to emulate, in his mature stage, the disciplined and dynamic realism of Pushkin himself.

Lermontov's unfinished realistic tale *Sashka* (1836) is an offspring mainly of Byron's *Don Juan* and, to some extent, of the first chapter of Pushkin's *Onegin*. It is a scathing and at times obscene satire against the provincial gentry in its process of moral decomposition. The realism of another tale in verse, *A Treasurer's Wife* (1837), written in the *Onegin* stanza, is modelled on Pushkin's *Count Nulin* and, through the latter, on Byron's *Beppo*. It gives a humorously caustic picture of provincial officials, one of whom gambles away his pretty wife to an army officer. At times Lermontov the realist actually reaches Pushkin's simplicity and detachment. In *Borodino* (1837), for example, he renders to perfection the tone, the manner and also the grumbling humour of an old veteran who talks to his grandson about Napoleon's first defeat during his invasion of Russia in 1812. And if the realism in some of his poems (such as his famous *Cossack Cradle Song*) can be poignantly touching, it acquires a dynamic matter-of-factness in the already mentioned picture of the battle on the Caucasian river Valerik—an anticipation of Tolstoy's battle scenes in *War and Peace*. The pathos of his *Testament* again is due to the discrepancy between the tragic situation of a soldier dying of wounds and the almost jokingly casual tone in which he tells his last wishes to a comrade due to go home on leave.

But if somebody questions you
About me as they may:
Just say that a certain bullet flew—
My chest was in the way;
Say I died bravely for the Tsar,
And say what fools our doctors are,
Tell them I send my duty
To Russia, home and beauty.

Mother and Dad—surely they still
Alive can scarce remain.
At any rate I'd hate to fill
Those old folks' days with pain.
But, if one of them lingers yet,
Just tell that there's no use to fret:
They've sent us to the fighting,
*And I'm no hand at writing.**

* Translated by V. de Sola Pinto.

The height of poetic detachment was reached, however, by Lermontov in a great work of a different order: his *Song about Tsar Ivan Vasilyevich, the Young Body-Guard and the Brave Merchant Kalashnikov*. This poem is the finest literary emulation of the historical folk-songs (similar to, yet not identical with the *byliny*). Here Lermontov came at least as close to the spirit of the people and to folk genius as Pushkin did in his poetic transposition of fairy-tales. But this is Lermontov at his best rather than his most typical. Essentially subjective, he succeeded only during the last period of his life in turning his personal moods and attitudes into great poetry, notably so when face to face with nature. This poem, the whole of which consists of one single sentence, can serve as a proof:

When o'er the yellowing corn a fleeting shadow rushes,
And fragrant forest glades re-echo in the breeze,
And in the garden's depths the ripe plum hides its blushes
Within the luscious shade of brightly verdant trees;

When bathed in scented dew, the silver lily,
At golden morn or evening shot with red,
From out behind a leafy bush peeps shyly,
And nods with friendly mien its dainty head;

When down the shady glen the bubbling streamlet dances,
And, lulling thought to sleep with its incessant song,
Lisps me the secrets, with a thousand glances,
Of that still corner where it speeds along;

Then does my troubled soul find solace for a while,
Then vanish for a time the furrows from my brow,
And happiness is mine a moment here below,
*And in the skies I see God smile.**

Pushkin would not have used so many adjectives and "purple patches" as Lermontov was wont to do, yet this does not mean that all his poems are full of them. Nor is he often as conciliatory as in the quoted lyric. His awareness of the difference between the world to which he is chained, and the timeless realm of his spirit is too painful to make him resigned to it. Besides, like so many romantics, he derived his poetic power principally from protest, rebellion, and that proud isolation which refuses to accept anything tainted with the stigma of the "human-all-too-human."

Oh gloomy and dreary! and no one to stretch out a hand
In hours when the soul nears disaster . . .
Desire! but what use is an empty desire without end?
And the years, the best years, but fly faster.

To love! yes, but whom? It is nothing in time's little space.
No love has an endless to-morrow!
Just look at yourself: what is past does not leave any trace.
They are nothing—both pleasure and sorrow.

What is passion? That sickness so sweet, either early or late,
Will vanish at reason's protesting;
And life, if you ever, attentive and cool, contemplate,
Is but empty and meaningless jesting.

* This poem, translated by Walter Morison, and the following, translated by C. M. Bowra, are taken from *A Book of Russian Verse* (Macmillan).

So the mood of *The Angel* keeps recurring in Lermontov's poetry like a permanent refrain to his own life. And since both his pessimism and his rebellion were due to metaphysical nostalgia, they often gave him that well-nigh elemental force of negation and challenge which came out in his two principal works, *The Novice* (1840) and *The Demon* (1841).

IV

THESE TWO TALES IN VERSE REPRESENT THE CLIMAX of Lermontov's romanticism and poetic genius in one. *The Novice*, in particular, is the most glowing assertion of freedom that ever came from under the pen of a Russian poet. Full of unsurpassed pictures of nature, it has nothing of the slow despondent rhythm of his famous *Meditation*, beginning with the line, "Sadly do I look upon our generation." The very pace of *The Novice* (he calls it in Georgian—*Mtsyri*) is so manly and bracing that there are no feminine endings in its four-footed iambics.* The theme itself goes back to Lermontov's early period. He began to work upon it in 1830. Five years later he embodied it as one of the motifs in his somewhat confused romantic tale in verse, *The Boyar Orsha*, and completed its final draft in the last year of his life. The tale is in the form of a confession on the part of a young

* Zhukovsky's excellent translation of Byron's *Prisoner of Chillon* was done (in 1821) in the same metre.

Caucasian mountaineer who as a child had been captured by the Russians and was then left in a Georgian monastery where he became a novice. But the monastery walls did not obliterate the memories of his childhood and his yearning for freedom. Determined to see his native place and to taste of a free life once again, he escapes, wanders amidst the gorgeous Caucasian scenery for days, but in the end is found dying of exhaustion and starvation not far from the spot where his adventure had started. Having thus completed the vicious circle, he is brought back to the monastery. He knows that his hours are numbered, but his spirit refuses to surrender. In words burning with passion he confesses to the old monk the reasons why he escaped and perseveres in his defiance to the end.

Tragic, but in a different sense, is Lermontov's "Eastern tale," *The Demon.* He had started working at it as far back as 1829 and 1830, took it up again in 1833, then during his stay in the Caucasus in 1837, and completed it (after several previous drafts) in 1841. The demon of this tale is Lermontov's own double, projected into the realm of the spirit. He is a rebellious exiled angel who still remembers his one-time bliss (*The Angel* motif again), but is doomed to be imprisoned in his own isolation till the end of time. The theme bears traces of Byron's influence—especially of his *Heaven and Earth*, of Thomas Moore's *The Love of Angels*, of *Eloa* by Alfred de Vigny, but in spite of this it remains Lermontov's most typical and personal creation. For it combines, in an intensified symbolic manner, all the features of his own nature: his feeling of loneliness, his rebellious pride, his secret wish as well as his inability to come to terms with life.

Unhappy Demon, spirit of exile,
Soared high above the sinful world,
And memories of the days of erstwhile
Before him brooding vision whirled,
Of days when in the light of grace
A cherub bright and pure he shone,
When in the swift, unending race
The comet turned its smiling face
To greet him as they fastened on ;
When through the everlasting gloaming,
Athirst of knowledge he pursued
The caravans of planets roaming
Through endless space without a goal,
When faith and love imbued his soul,
The happy first-born of creation,
Unknown to fear or pride's inflation,
Nor came to haunt his limpid mind
The threat of endless years of pain . . .
And much, so much he strove to find
*Deep in his memory, but in vain.**

And since this is an "Eastern tale," the Caucasus—the Russian romantic East—is introduced as the only adequate background for a spirit of such stature. It is the Caucasus Lermontov had known and admired since his boyhood.

* All the passages are taken from Gerard Shelley's translation of *The Demon* (The Richards Press).

Then o'er the high Caucasian maze
The banished angel slowly rose,
Kazbek with glinting lights ablaze,
Stood clad in everlasting snows.
And deep below, an inky track
Like a dark serpent's hiding-crack,
The winding Darial met his gaze.
The Terek like a lion bounding
With shaggy mane upon the peak
Set all the hollow vales resounding ;
And beasts upon the mountain bleak
And birds aloft in heaven's light
Both harkened to its thundered word ;
And golden clouds in endless flight
Sped with it northward undeterred.

The beauty of Gruzia or Georgia, embedded in that scenery, is

Spread out in glittering, gorgeous views,
Ablaze with morning's rosy dews,
With lofty ruins ivy-decked
And purling brooks that flow unchecked
O'er beds of multi-coloured stones.

It is amidst the most beautiful views in the world that the Demon suddenly beholds Tamara—the most beautiful of mortals, and falls in love with her. But Tamara, already betrothed, is expecting the arrival of her bridegroom who, accompanied by a whole caravan, hurries to the wedding. Tamara and her girl-friends while away the time with innocent pleasures.

And on the roof in rich array
The bride sits with her maiden throng,
Filling the hours with play and song
Till o'er the distant hills the day
Warns them that night will not be long.
Their palms in gentle measure clapping,
They sing, and then the young bride takes
Her tambourine, which, gently tapping
Above her head, she gaily shakes
With a lily hand that faintly quakes.
Now lighter than a bird she dashes,
Then, pausing, she will fix her gaze
While two moist eyes are seen to blaze
Beneath their jealous tapering lashes ;
Now she will raise her brows with pride,
Now suddenly her form incline,
Then o'er the patterned floor will glide
Her foot so lovely, so divine !
And oft her face will sweetly smile
With gentle mirth devoid of guile.
A beam of moonlight faintly trembling
Upon the ruffled water's face,
Though much her wreathed smile resembling,
Can scarce compare for light or grace.

The Demon sees to it that the caravan of the wedding guests is dispersed, while the bridegroom himself is killed. In despair, Tamara retires to a convent, but here the Demon begins to tempt her in her dreams. He does this with no evil intentions, for Tamara's beauty has made such a profound change in him that he actually hopes his love for her might save him at last from isolation and even reconcile him to God and His world. Invisible, he whispers to her:

The gentle prayer of love unending
I bring to thee with heart aglow,
On earth my spirit's first unbending,
The first tears from my eyes to flow.
O let them not unheeded go!
Heaven knows that one word of thine
Can make my simple soul surrender,
And clad in thy love's light divine
In Paradise again I'd shine
Like a new angel in new splendour.

But this is not granted to him. When, finally, he embraces Tamara, she dies from the kiss of an immortal. Her soul is taken away by a messenger of God. The Demon is left in the same cosmic loneliness as ever.

Again he roamed in desolation,
The haughty exile of creation,
On whom no hope or love shall gleam.

In spite of its somewhat operatic theme and setting, this poem remains one of the masterpieces of Russian literature. Lermontov expressed in it symbolically the depth of his own uprootedness as only a romantic of his brand could have done. Yet the plane of such poetry was too vague, too far removed from the actualities of the day and the conditions of an entire generation lost as it were in the desert of Russian life under Nicholas I. So he decided to tackle the problem from a different angle and in prose; which he did in his novel, *A Hero of our Time* (1840).

LERMONTOV

V

ALTHOUGH LERMONTOV HIMSELF WARNS US, IN THE preface to the second edition of this work, not to confuse Pechorin—the hero of the novel—with the personality of the author, we cannot but think that he analysed in it above all his own negative features. But in portraying himself, he portrayed also the generation to which he belonged. In this manner he wrote his counterpart to Alfred de Musset's *La Confession d'un enfant du siècle*, a book he must have been hardly less familiar with than he was with *Adolphe* by Benjamin Constant. Like the two works mentioned, *A Hero of our Time* is a psychological novel, and its importance is further enhanced by the fact that it is written in a prose as perfect and lucid as the prose of Pushkin, but at the same time even more flexible.

Pechorin himself is a literary descendant of Pushkin's Onegin, but he is an Onegin of the 'thirties : intensified, psychologically dissected and presented to the reader as the new up-to-date variety of the "superfluous" man. A preliminary portrait of Pechorin can be found in Lermontov's unfinished early novel, *Princess Ligovskaya* (1836), where he combines self-analysis with a picture of the rather callous Petersburg society, with its indifference towards social inferiors. But what was here only a sketch and a promise, became in *A Hero of our Time* a fulfilment. Consisting of five parts, all of which can be read independently, this masterpiece shows in the first two narratives (*Bela*, *Maxim Maximych*) Pechorin as he is seen by others, and in the subsequent three parts (*Taman*, *Princess Mary*, *The Fatalist*) as he sees and describes himself in his own diary. The background is for the most part the Caucasus again ; only the incidents of *Taman* (one of the best stories in Russian) is set in the Crimea.

The final impression Pechorin makes upon the reader is one of a tragic failure. He has all the marks of a strong and superior nature, but can never apply his strength to anything worth his while, since in the Russia of that period no creative outlet was provided or even possible for people of his calibre. All his potential strength thus turns against itself and becomes vindictively destructive. The more so because he is a hidden idealist by nature, whereas by conviction he is a sceptic unable to believe in any ideals. Devoid of an adequate creative task or mission, he is doomed to remain negative in whatever he does. "I have never been able to discover my mission," he confesses, "so I have succumbed to the temptation of futile and ungrateful passions. Out of their furnace I have issued hard and cold as steel, but I have hopelessly failed to pluck the most beautiful flower of life—the fire of noble impulses. How often have I been no more than an axe in the hands of fate. Like a death-dealing instrument, I fell upon the heads of the predestined victims, often without angry feelings, but always without regret."

Pechorin is in other ways, too, a rather split, "modern" personality. He is full of the will to live, to enjoy, while, at the same time, his sceptical reason continually watches, analyses and undermines his best impulses. Such a division makes him increasingly self-conscious, until the only intense feeling still accessible to him is that of his power, which he duly exercises as an end in itself. Other people, especially women (Bela, Vera, Princess Mary) whom he fascinates, become deplorable victims of the power he has over them. He himself is aware of this, painfully aware at times, and the only thing in his favour is that he has at least the honesty to acknowledge it. "I see the sufferings and the joys of others only in relation to myself; I regard them as food to nourish my spiritual strength," he says further in his diary. "It has become impossible for me to do foolish deeds under the influence of passion. In me, ambition has been crushed by circumstances, to assume another form. For ambition is nothing but the thirst for power, and my chief delight is to impose my will upon all with whom I come in contact. To inspire fear, what is it but the first sign and the greatest triumph of power? To be for some one a cause of suffering or joy, without the least right—can pride know sweeter food than this?" No wonder Pechorin himself comes to the conclusion: "Substantially I was a cripple."*

VI

STRENGTH, DOOMED TO BE FRUSTRATED, TO TURN against itself or else to degenerate into the nihilistic

* Translated by Eden and Cedar Paul (Allen & Unwin).

"will to power"—such was the inner tragedy of Lermontov's own personality. Through his masterly analysis of this tragedy Lermontov deepened the problem of the "superfluous man" and thus became the creator of the psychological novel in Russian literature. He was the first to tackle some of those aspects of individual frustration which afterwards were further developed in Dostoevsky's writings.

Even the "demoniac" pride and self-assertiveness of Dostoevsky's complex heroes, such as Raskolnikov and Stavrogin, have some of their roots in Lermontov. Whereas one aspect of Dostoevsky's work goes back to Gogol, the other points to Lermontov, and via Lermontov to Byron—however distant the affinities may be at times.

As a painter of the "superfluous man" Lermontov forms a link between Pushkin on the one hand, and Turgenev and Goncharov on the other. As a psychologist, however, he leads to Dostoevsky. By his frankness and his refusal to indulge in any shams or rosy spectacles, he, moreover, introduced into Russian literature that psychological and moral honesty which often verged on recklessness. Both as poet and novelist, Lermontov inaugurated the vertical direction in Russian literature. It was he who made it *conscious* of depth (which is something different from the unconscious depth) at a time when the more horizontal "natural school" was already branching off into a number of those aspects which formed the basis of the subsequent Russian realism.

FOUR

Fyodor Tyutchev

I

AMONG THE LEADING FIGURES IN RUSSIAN LITERATURE, the poet Fyodor Tyutchev (1803-73) is still hardly a name in Western Europe. But this is not surprising —even in Russia it took two or three generations before his work was appreciated at its true value. As his early poems coincided with the Pushkin period, he is often mentioned rightly or wrongly among the members of the Pushkin *pléiade*. Some of his best verses actually appeared in Pushkin's periodical *The Contemporary* (*Sovremennik*) in 1836, i.e. while Pushkin was still alive. Apart from this, however, Tyutchev had no close contacts with that group. Besides, on leaving the Moscow University at the age of nineteen, he was attached, almost at once, to the Russian Legation in Munich and later to that in Turin. His stay abroad lasted some twenty-two years, during which his genius reached its maturity away from his native land and largely under foreign influences.

The city he for several reasons liked and enjoyed

most was Munich, which King Ludwig I, himself a poet, succeeded in turning—at least for a while—into a lively meeting-ground for writers, artists and cultural workers in general. Tyutchev felt thoroughly at home in such an atmosphere and made good use of it. Nor did he neglect stimulating personal contacts. In 1828 he was in touch with Heinrich Heine who in a letter refers to him as his "best Munich friend." In the same year he often saw Schelling whose philosophy of nature, together with Goethe's pantheism, exercised a strong influence upon his poetry. As Tyutchev's second wife had lived in Weimar where she had known Goethe, it is possible that Tyutchev, too, had met him personally, but this is only a conjecture. Anyway, when in 1832 Goethe died, his Russian admirer dedicated to him a poem worthy of its subject.

Tyutchev was not a prolific writer. The total number of poems to his credit is somewhere between 450 and 500. Considering the fact that he reached the age of seventy, this is not a great deal. He felt, moreover, rather indifferent to his literary career. It is significant that on his return to Petersburg, in 1844, he soon became famous as a brilliant society wit and causeur, whereas his poems were known only to the initiated. Refusing to curry favour either with the critics or with the readers, he had to wait until 1850 for the first competent appreciation (by the poet Nekrasov) of his work. But even after that he showed so little interest in the promise of a belated literary fame that he took no part in the first printed collection of his poems in 1854 and left it entirely to the discretion of his friend, the novelist I. S. Turgenev. The truth is that he wrote only under inner compulsion, i.e. when he could not help it, and even then with apparent reluctance. For he realised the inadequacy of the spoken or written words and felt sceptical about them. In one of his finest poems, *Silentium*, he explains the reason for his own meagre output in these lines, known to every lover of Russian poetry :

Heart knows not to speak with heart.
Song and speech can ne'er impart
Faith by which we live and die.
A thought once spoken is a lie.
Unbroken, undefiled, unstirred
*Thy fountain : drink and say no word.**

Fortunately, Tyutchev did not always adhere to such an injunction. There were moments when he could not abstain from singing, whether he wanted or not. His intimate contact with Nature was responsible for a number of those moments. So was his emotionalised thought, aroused by his intense and disturbingly visionary cosmic feeling. The spell of a tragic love which swayed him in his old age was responsible for a last and final crop of excellent lyrics. And since he sang only when he had to, he put into his verses all the artistic and human integrity of which he was capable. Turgenev once said that Tyutchev's poems are not redolent of anything laboured, but seem to have been written, as Goethe wrote, on the spur of certain moments, and instead of having been

* Translated by R. M. Hewitt in *A Book of Russian Verse* (Macmillan).

made, have grown of their own accord "like the fruits on a tree."

II

TO THE AVERAGE POETRY-READER IN RUSSIA TYUTCHEV is known mainly on account of his nature lyrics. These are less ethereal but more direct and incisive in their laconic impressionism than the lyrics of his younger contemporary, Afanasy Fet. They are also imbued with frequent philosophic contemplation spontaneously arising out of his moods rather than imposed upon them. He may sing about plains and mountains, spring floods, sea-waves, seasons, mornings and evenings—the array of motifs used by thousands of poets before him ; yet he does it in his own manner, and his voice can be recognised without mistake. As a rule, he selects a few details only which he arranges in such a way as to suggest the whole picture in its most striking aspects by a minimum of means. Even such an obvious nature poem as his *Spring Storm*, known from textbooks to every Russian schoolboy, can serve as an example. It begins with the simplest lines imaginable :

I like a storm at May's beginning,
When Spring's first thunder with wild cries
As though in frolic gaily spinning
Rumbles all round the pale blue skies.

The elements of the storm are then compressed into eight lines only, but sufficient to show it in its fullness, with the "jargon of the forests, brawl of the mountains —all gaily echoing the thunder's roar." A mental picture with an appropriate simile is added as a final touch and conclusion :

Hebe, you'd say, had seized a brimming
Cup from Jove's eagle in wild mirth,
And with laughter had dashed the swimming
*Nectar from heaven across the earth.**

But Tyutchev's lyrics are not always as cheerful as in the poem above. His impressionism often assumes a disquieting meditative character, tinged with a symbolic meaning. The symbolist and the impressionist methods generally tend to converge in him and to strengthen each other—containing now and then a summing-up comment as they do at the end of these verses:

The light of autumn evening seems a screen,
Some mystery with tender glamour muffling. . . .
The trees in motley, cloaked and eerie sheen,
The scarlet leaves that languid airs are ruffling,
The still and misty azure, vaguely far,
Above the earth that waits her orphan sorrow,
And bitter winds in gusty fragrance are
Forerunners of a bleak, storm-driven morrow.
The woods are waning ; withered is the sun ;
Earth shows the smile of passing, meekly tender
As the grave shyness of the suffering one,
*In noble reticence of sad surrender.**

The last three lines stress the symbolic kernel of the

* Translated by V. de Sola Pinto.

† Translated by Babette Deutsch and Avrahm Yarmolinsky in *Russian Poetry* (Lawrence).

picture. The symbolism of the following motif— a willow leaning over the running water—is, however, transparent enough to explain itself without any comment:

Why, O willow, to the river
Leans thy head so low, and why
Dost thou with long leaves that tremble
And that thirsty lips resemble
Catch the ripples dancing by?
Though thy leaflets faint and quiver,
Mirrored in the fleeting stream,
Yet the current speeds and splashes,
In caressing sunshine flashes,
*And but mocks thy empty dream.**

In Pushkin's poetry the phenomena of nature exist as a rule in their own right, i.e. objectively, and are described as such. Tyutchev, on the other hand, prefers to approach them either as vehicles of his own moods and thoughts, or else to look upon them as a cover of what is clandestinely working behind and beyond it all. He did not neglect nature poems pure and simple. Yet his most original contributions to Russian literature are those verses in which nature itself is symbolically interpreted—as a veil hiding from man's eyes the deeper cosmic processes active at the root of all being.

It was here in particular that certain influences of German thought left their mark in Tyutchev's work. Under the impact of Goethe's pantheism and even more of Schelling's philosophy of the identity between Spirit and the Universe, he came to consider Nature as

* Translated by Walter Morison in *A Book of Russian Verse* (Macmillan).

a living organism—with a soul, a mind and a language of its own. These are accessible, however, to man in the moment when the clarity of the day is replaced by the irrational element of the night. During the day we see the surface of Nature in all her alluring but deceptive beauty. Only when the day is gone can man's consciousness be attuned to the darker mysteries coming from the depth of being. He is then able to partake of universal life, provided he surrenders to it to the point of forgetting or even obliterating his own *moi haïssable*. Such pantheistic moods at the hour of approaching night are well rendered in Tyutchev's *Twilight* :

Dove-blue shades have met and mingled,
Colours fade and sound is sleeping—
Life and movement all dissolve in
Trembling twilight, far-off weeping.
Moths upon their unseen journeys
Murmuring through the darkness fall . . .
Moment this of wordless yearning !
All within me, I in all. . . .

Gentle twilight, sleepy twilight,
Penetrate my inmost soul,
Tranquil, languid, full of odours,
All suffusing, lulling all !
In a mist of self-oblivion
Every feeling softly fold !
Let me taste annihilation,
*Merge me with the sleeping world.**

* Translated by Walter Morison.

Night and twilight, imbued with this quasi-mystical flavour, became Tyutchev's favourite motifs. Appealing to his cosmic sense rather than to his sense of nature, they affected him accordingly. What during the day appeared as harmony and beauty, was bound to dissolve at night into the foreboding of chaos as the lurking primeval core of the universe. If the beauty of nature gave him moments of ecstasy, the magic of night, charged with the bigger mystery of the cosmos, filled him with *angoisse* and metaphysical horror. His pantheism thus assumed the dualistic aspect of Day and Night, the symbolic meaning of which he expresses in this key-poem :

Across the spirits' secret world,
Hiding the chaos and the void,
The great gods, lest we be destroyed,
A golden curtain have unfurled.
This radiant veil we call the Day,
The lustrous Day, whose golden weave
Gleams nimbus-like on all who grieve,
And jewels with his joys the gay.

But Day wanes : Night shrouded in dusk,
Stalks forward, and with gestures gruff
Crumbles and rends the precious stuff,
And casts it down like any husk.
Then the abyss is bared to sight,
Its terrors grim, its shadows vast ;
We shrink back, desperate, aghast.
*Hence men, beholding fear the Night.**

* Translated by Babette Deutsch and Avrahm Yarmolinsky. Op. cit.

FYODOR TYUTCHEV

III

AROUND THE HACKNEYED ANTITHESIS OF DAY AND night Tyutchev wove some of his boldest imagery, but always with the emphasis on the night. The poetry of night was in vogue among the romantics, especially in Germany where it had such votaries as Novalis, Tieck, Eichendorff and others. Yet it would be hard to find a poet who knew how to render this "shrinking back aghast" with such force as Tyutchev. If one can speak of "nocturnal" metaphysics at all, we find it in his verses which are utterly devoid of any sentimentality often connected with such moods. Moreover, it was not terror alone but also the fascination of the Night that drew him irresistibly with its mystery and magic.

As ocean's stream girdles the ball of earth,
From circling seas of dream man's life emerges,
And as night moves in silence up the firth
The secret tide around our mainland surges.

The voice of urgent waters softly sounds ;
The magic skiff uplifts white wings of wonder.
The tide swells swiftly and the white sail rounds,
Where the blind waves in shoreless darkness thunder.

And the wide heavens, starred and luminous,
Out of the deep in mystery aspire.
The strange abyss is burning under us ;
*And we sail onwards, and our wake is fire.**

* Translated by Babette Deutsch and Avrahm Yarmolinsky. Op. cit.

FYODOR TYUTCHEV

Tyutchev's awe of the waves thundering in the "shoreless darkness" instead of abating as time went on, only grew stronger. He felt lost and forlorn like an orphan in the face of it, and while singing of man's "fateful heritage," often obliterated the dividing line between things visual and things visionary. His impressionism passed into a strangely realistic symbolism.

The night was dark with indignation ;
With cloud the sky was shrouded deep ;
It was not threat nor meditation,
But drugged uncomfortable sleep.

Only the lightning's summer revels
Flashed alternating, out and in,
As if a horde of deaf-mute devils
Were holding conference of sin.

As if a sign agreed were given,
Broad conflagration fired the sky,
And momently from the dark heaven
Woods and far forests met the eye.

Then disappeared again the vision ;
In visible darkness all was pent
As if some great and dire decision
*Were taken in the firmament.**

"A horde of deaf-mute devils holding conference of sin" is one of those pregnant phrases (Tyutchev's poetry is full of them) which, once read, cannot be forgotten. Yet as an emanation of his *angoisse*, it also

* Translated by Anon. in *A Book of Russian Verse* (Macmillan).

points to realities within his own mind by which he was haunted. For he found there the same conflicting tendencies as in the cosmic life at large, only more personal, more painful—with the chaotic "nocturnal" element frequently on top.

Oh, thou, my wizard soul, oh, heart
That whelming agony immerses,
The threshold of two universes
In cleaving these, tears thee apart.†

Self-division of this kind anticipated certain traits of the *fin de siècle.* The "agony" alluded to was rendered even more unbearable because of the threat of scepticism to which he was no stranger. As far back as in 1851, he described to perfection (in eight lines) the inner vacuum resulting from that scepticism which was doomed to undermine the generation of the "moderns."

No sickness of the flesh is ours to-day
Whose time is spent in grieving and despairing ;
Who pray all night that night will pass away—
Who greet the dawn rebelliously uncaring.

Withered and parched by unbelief, the soul
Impossible, unbearable things is bearing.
We are lost men, and ruin is our goal,
*Athirst for faith, to beg for faith not daring.**

Tyutchev, too, was in danger of being inwardly paralysed by such a state of mind, and he knew it. In fact, during the decade preceding the above verses he

† Translated by Babette Deutsch and Avrahm Yarmolinsky. Op. cit.
* Translated by R. Christie in *A Book of Russian Verse* (Macmillan).

wrote surprisingly little. He might have become silent altogether, had not chance provided him with a new source of inspiration. What happened was that in 1850 Tyutchev, a married middle-aged man holding a high post in the department of censorship, fell passionately in love with a certain Mlle Denisyeva—a niece of the headmistress of the exclusive Smolny Institute, where his daughters were educated. Far from being a mere Platonic affair, this love lasted some fourteen years (until Mlle Denisyeva's death in 1864) and had a profound effect on Tyutchev's life and work.

IV

THERE HAVE BEEN MANY POETS OF FIRST LOVE, BUT Tyutchev is not one of them. He sings of his last love instead. And his melancholy is not one of joy but of the nostalgic sadness of a parting day, the very beauty of which is tragic, as we can easily gather from his poem, *Last Love* :

As our years sink away, how tender it grows,
Our love, and how filled with fateful boding . . .
Shine on us, shine, thou farewell glow
Of love's last ray, of the twilight's brooding.

Shades have reft half the sky away :
Westward alone the light still lingers.
Bide with us, charm of the dying day ;
Withdraw not, enchantment, thy magic fingers !

Let the coursing blood grow thin as gall,
If the heart but keep its tender burning . . .
O last and latest love of all,
*Thou art bliss unending, and hopeless yearning.**

Tragic in its own way was also the love of Mlle Denisyeva. The ambiguous position of a pretty young woman who gave birth to three illegitimate children while her lover's German wife was still alive, by no means made things easy for her. The gossip, slander, social ostracism she had to endure, can be imagined. Nor was Tyutchev himself always as tender as he says. There were times when his moods and temper became unbearable. Besides, neither of the two lovers seemed to be able to separate love from torment and subsequent self-torment. A lyric in which he gives a condensed history of his last passion begins with the frank exclamation, "Oh, how killingly we love ; how in the reckless blindness of passions we are sure to ruin all that is dear to our heart !" The "immortal vulgarity of men," having chosen Mlle Denisyeva for its target, did the rest. And the result ? Two wrecked lives, and a series of the most poignant love-lyrics in Russian literature. These are written in a realistic vein, with a frequent colloquial inflection. In some of them Tyutchev castigates himself by putting into the mouth of his beloved grave accusations, as though the verses had been written not by him but by her—in order to indict him.

* Translated by Walter Morison.

That, as before, he loves me, tell me never,
Nor that he treasures me as in the days gone by . . .
Oh no! My life's thin thread, he, ruthless seeks to sever,
For all I see the blade his fingers ply.

Now raging, now in tears, with grief and anger seething,
Swept madly on, my soul plucked bare and raw,
I ache, nor am alive . . . in him alone know breathing;
And needle-sharp is every breath I draw.

He measures me the air more grudgingly and sparsely
Than one would mete it out to one's most hated foe.
I still can breathe; though painfully and harshly,
*I still draw breath—but life no longer know.**

The contrition after each fit of harshness may have increased the depth and the sincerity of his more tender feelings, but the continuous ups and downs of this kind were costly for both—emotionally and physically. After some fourteen years of such love, it was the woman who had to pay the ultimate price. A glimpse of her agony can be obtained from this poem:

All day unconscious she was lying there,
And evening shadows came and wrapt her round;
Warm summer rain fell soft upon the leaves
In steady flow and made a cheerful sound.

And slowly she returned into herself,
And trained her sense the pleasant sound to hear,
And listened long, her mind absorbed in thought
That carried her away, yet left her near.

* Translated by Walter Morison.

Then, as one speaking to herself, alone,
Now conscious of the sound and all beside
(I watched her, yet alive, though death was near)
"How dearly have I loved all this!" she sighed.

Oh how thou loved'st it! And to love like thee
Has to no other in the world been given!
My God! and can I then my death survive
*And my poor heart in fragments not be riven?**

Her death was an irreparable blow to Tyutchev. "Only in her presence was I a personality, only in her love, her boundless love for me, was I aware of myself," he owned to one of his friends in October 1864. "Now I am a meaningless, painfully living nonentity." Before long his poetic gift, too, began to decline. But while his lyrical vein seemed to be in abeyance, there was a sudden increase in the output of his political and civic verses—the last group of his poetry still to be considered.

V

WITH VERY FEW EXCEPTIONS, TYUTCHEV'S POLITICAL poems cannot be compared either in depth or in technique with his lyrics. They are primarily a register of the ideological attitudes typical of Tyutchev the Russian and the aristocrat. His earliest political poem—an answer to Pushkin's *Ode to Liberty*—goes back to

* Translated by P. E. Matheson in *Holy Russia and Other Poems* (Oxford University Press).

1820. Tyutchev wrote it in the liberal spirit prevalent among the advanced aristocratic youths of that generation. Later, however, he changed his opinions and after the Paris rebellion in 1830, definitely sided with reaction and with the ideas of the Holy Alliance. He also became an ardent Russian patriot (while still continuing to use in private conversation and correspondence French in preference to his native tongue). In 1841 he, moreover, paid a visit to Prague, whence he returned a convinced pan-Slavist of the Russian brand.

Russia was considered by him, from now on, the only guarantee for the old order, since the West seemed to be in a constant fermentation which reached its climax in the revolutions of 1848. As a scion of the old serf-owning nobility, he was so frightened of the revolutionary trend and movements in Europe that he wrote four essays (in French) in order to enlighten the world at large. The most important of these essays is *La Russe et la Revolution* (1849), and the gist of it was summed up by him in one of his best political poems, *The Rock and the Sea*, in which Tsarist Russia is likened to a cliff surrounded by the waves of the revolution vainly dashing against its "gigantic heel."

In spite of his one-time friendship with Heine, Tyutchev now turned his back on everything men of Heine's stamp were fighting for. Having identified Europe with the revolution, he prophesied in verse and in prose the "decline of the West" and propped up his imperialistic pan-Slavism with a rather sophisticated philosophy of history. Russia would, in his opinion, eventually become the leader of all the Slavs, and the universal monarchy she was destined to found would extend as far as Nile and Ganges, with Constantinople as its capital. A *pax russica* would then stem for ever the fury of the revolution, fomented by the "godless" masses of the West. In his poem, *Sunrise,* he gives an allegorical utterance to the adage, *ex oriente lux*—quite in the spirit of militant Slavophilism. Little did he suspect that about a hundred years later the irony of history would make a socialist Russia lead all the Slavs towards a revolutionised pattern of existence, whereas the European West would desperately try to save what still could be saved of the old order. It was for patriotic rather than religious reasons that Tyutchev now stressed also his allegiance to the Russian Orthodox Church. In one of his poems he mentions Christ wandering in a slave's garb all over Russia and bestowing blessings upon her—a symbol of that Messianism which was so dear to the older Slavophils.

The setbacks of the Russian army during the Crimean Campaign had a sobering effect upon Tyutchev. The morass into which the corrupt bureaucracy had plunged the country was something of a revelation to him, and when Nicholas I died (during the campaign) Tyutchev frankly said in a poem what he thought of the defunct sovereign. For whatever his prejudices, Tyutchev was not a time-server. Even his patriotism was sincere. But as he viewed the destinies of his country through his semi-feudal and imperialist spectacles, he was bound to see everything in a wrong perspective. One more proof that good poets are rarely good politicians.

FYODOR TYUTCHEV

VI

TYUTCHEV'S PLACE AMONG THE GREATEST RUSSIAN poets is no longer contested. Dostoevsky once called him the first poet-philosopher in Russian literature, and Tolstoy, who otherwise cared little for poetry, rated Tyutchev higher than Pushkin. Touching with one end of his development the classical eighteenth century of Derzhavin, he anticipated with the other end the Russian school of symbolism. He was a "modern" before time. This may have been one of the reasons why he had to wait so long for recognition. For in spite of the high tribute paid to him by such contemporaries as Nekrasov, Turgenev, Apollon Grigoryev, and even the ultra-radical critic Dobrolyubov, Tyutchev's work came into its own only towards the end of the last century.

The pioneering article by the philosopher and poet Vladimir Solovyov (in 1895) was followed by a crop of essays in which some of the leading Russian symbolists proclaimed Tyutchev one of their predecessors. The climax of his vogue was reached, however, in 1913, when a complete edition of his works, prefaced by one of the leading modernists, Valery Bryusov, was launched as a supplement to the most widely spread monthly, *Niva* (The Cornfield). Nor did it suffer an eclipse after the Revolution of 1917. In spite of his political views, he is relished as a poet by Soviet readers. Amongst the recent editions of his works there is a large one even for Soviet children—surely a sign of popularity which is almost reaching danger point.

FIVE

Ivan Turgenev

I

IVAN TURGENEV WAS THE FIRST RUSSIAN AUTHOR TO become generally known and admired beyond the boundaries of his own country. It was through him that Russian fiction began to penetrate into Europe as one of the major literary influences, and for good reason, since he always knew how to combine his "Russianness" with impeccable literary manners and with a technique perfect enough to challenge comparison with any great prose-writer of the West. He loses only if compared with such cyclopic geniuses as Dostoevsky and Tolstoy who can afford to be a law unto themselves. Similarly in the world of music, Mozart seems to lose if compared with Beethoven, for example : but while Beethoven may be a greater genius, Mozart remains a greater artist.

Turgenev belongs to what might be called the well-ordered Mozartian—or, for that matter, Pushkinian—type of creators. Whatever subject he took on, he handled it first of all as a perfect artist. External reality, including its most topical aspects and problems, was for him but raw material which he distilled into works of beauty. Keenly interested in political, social and cultural struggles of the day, he had his own definite convictions, sympathies, antipathies ; yet he never let them interfere with the aesthetic side of his writings. This did not exclude, of course, that unconscious interference which determines beforehand as it were one's choice of certain themes and characters in preference to others. In this respect Turgenev was a descendant of the old "nests of gentlefolk" at the very height of the intelligentsia period of Russian culture and literature. Although himself a member of the intelligentsia and a sincere liberal with a Western outlook, he yet remained a Russian nobleman with the ancestral country-house not only in his memory but in his very blood. In contrast to the more radical intellectuals who came from the "commoners" and looked only towards the future, Turgenev the artist could not help being rooted in the past even when fighting it in the light of the vital problems of the day. The company of the impetuous "commoners," so conspicuous in the ranks of the intelligentsia during the 'sixties, hardly made him feel quite at ease. At any rate, when at the beginning of that momentous decade a split between the "gentlemen" and the "commoners" took place within the precincts of *The Contemporary* itself (the principal organ of the advanced intelligentsia), Turgenev was one of those who walked out of the editorial premises.

After that split, the "commoners"—under the leadership of Dobrolyubov and Chernyshevsky—practically monopolised the journalistic and pamphleteering activities, whereas the "gentlemen" concentrated more on literature proper. With the exception of Dostoevsky and Leskov, both of whom were of mixed origin, the principal authors of the 'fifties, 'sixties and 'seventies, dealt mostly with the country-house and the village. This applies above all to Turgenev, whose work can perhaps be defined as the swan-song of a class which had a past but could no longer look forward with confidence to a future. It is against the background of this class, with its prevalent moods, that we can best see Turgenev's life and work in their right perspective.

II

TURGENEV WAS BORN IN 1818 IN THE DISTRICT OF OREL. Having lost his father while still a boy, he was at the mercy of a tyrannical mother. It was probably Turgenev's hatred for his mother that made him loathe, since boyhood, that system in which such irresponsible autocrats were still possible. After his education at home he studied at the University of Moscow, then in St. Petersburg, and finally in Berlin (1838-41), where he came into contact with Western culture and was so favourably impressed by it as to remain a convinced "Westerner" to the end of his days. On his return from abroad he started writing poetry and achieved considerable success with his tale in verse *Parasha* (1843), influenced by both Pushkin and Lermontov. He seemed to waver, for a while, between poetry, drama and fiction. His plays, such as the now famous *A Month in the Country* (1850) and *A Provincial Lady* (1851), are not devoid of originality, especially the first which, in its own way, anticipated the dramatic technique of Chekhov. But an even more startling new note was brought by Turgenev into prose—by those stories and jottings of his which began to appear in 1847 and were issued in book form in 1852 under the title, *A Sportsman's Sketches*.

Such a title looked innocent and reassuring: just a collection of impressions recorded by a roaming sportsman. Yet in the process of reading one becomes aware of the actual theme of the book—the serf and the squire. For the first time we meet here the serf in his everyday surroundings and in his normal everyday contacts with the serf-owner. As the liberation of the serfs was then generally expected, such a theme was topical at the time and had already been introduced in a sentimental-humanitarian manner (quite in the spirit of the "natural school") by Grigorovich. But in contrast to Grigorovich's *Village* or *Anton Goremyka*, Turgenev followed only his own artistic instinct, even when dealing with such a topical theme as serfdom. Without distorting either the truth of life or that of art by any sentimental considerations, he depicted a great variety of serfs and peasants simply as human beings in their own right, with their own ways of thinking, and with their own individual defects and virtues on a par with everybody else. The same balanced objectivity comes out in his portraits of the landowners, and it was not Turgenev's fault if many of these seemed to be humanly less valuable than their serfs. The whole of it expands into a mosaic of Russian rural life, and some of his pictures—the exquisitely drawn children in *Bezhin Meadow*, or the story called *The Singers*, for example—are unforgettable. So are Turgenev's landscapes. He knows how to be impressive through reserve and never takes liberties with Nature. Hence his preference for the nuance and for that discreet lyrical intimacy with the rural scenery in which the mellowness of colour and of verbal music serves as an evocative accompaniment to the atmosphere demanded by the situation. Turgenev's scenery is no longer a mere background for the characters—it merges with them as an indispensable part of the action itself. The Russian countryside has thus found in him its best "impressionistic" interpreter. With regard to his characters, too, Turgenev is above all an observer with an incredibly sharp eye for those significant trifles through which he can describe a person or a whole crowd of people by a minimum of means. This is how he introduces the hero of one of his sketches: "His face, plump and round as a ball, expressed bashfulness, good-natured and humble meekness: his nose, also plump and round and streaked with blue veins, betokened a sensualist. On the front of his head there was not a single hair left, some thin brown tufts stuck out behind; there was an ingratiating twinkle in his little eyes, set in long slits, and a sweet smile on his red, juicy lips. He had on a coat with a stand-up collar and brass buttons, very worn but clean ; his cloth trousers were hitched up high, his fat calves were visible above the yellow tops of his boots."

As his observation is never dissociated from experience, we see his characters as living realities and seem to know them intimately—as though we had lived with them for years. With the same balanced sensibility he tackles social and political problems without preaching, i.e. without making any compromises with his artistic conscience. Paradoxically enough, it was this trait in particular that enhanced the social and moral appeal of *A Sportsman's Sketches*. By exposing the iniquity and the cruelties of the serfdom system only as an artist and not as a preacher, he made the implied but sublimated social-humanitarian "purpose" all the more tangible by the magic of his art. Anyway, when the sketches appeared in book-form, they made such a strong impression on the Tsarevich himself (the prospective Tsar Alexander II) as to increase his determination to abolish serfdom—a conspicuous example of the influence of art upon history.

III

TURGENEV'S VISION, LIKE THAT OF PUSHKIN, IS ALWAYS concrete. He remains an observer even when he is introspective: in his *Diary of a Superfluous Man*, for instance, or in *Smoke*. As Henry James put it in one of his notes, he "has no recognition of unembodied ideas ; an idea, with him, is such and such a nose and chin, such and such a hat and waistcoat, bearing the same relation to it as the look of the printed word does to its meaning." And Turgenev himself said in a paper that he "had never attempted to create a type without having, not an idea, but a living person, in whom the various elements were harmonised together, to work from." In contrast to Dostoevsky, whose genius was more visionary than visual and therefore saw all characters mainly from within ; or to Tolstoy, who knew how to combine his clairvoyant eye and his incredible plastic power with an adequate analysis, Turgenev confined himself to the surface, but without ever being superficial. His characters are as much alive as any of those created by Tolstoy and Dostoevsky, although their range may be smaller and less ambitious. Unlike many Russian authors, Turgenev was endowed with quite a rare sense of construction, proportion, and of a carefully worked out—if never very complicated—plot. All these things he perfected by learning from Pushkin and Lermontov rather than from Gogol. The first two stories he wrote, *Andrey Kolosov* (1844) and *A Reckless Fellow* (1847), bear the stamp of Pechorin in Lermontov's *A Hero of our Time*. In another and considerably later story, *Knock, Knock, Knock* (1870), he gave a parody of the same character. Even in *A Sportsman's Sketches*, several of which are just carefully worked out "slices" of life, one cannot but admire that architectonic sense of his which achieved veritable triumphs in his later and bigger stories, and especially in his novels: *Rudin* (1855), *A Nest of Gentlefolk* (1858), *On the Eve* (1860), *Fathers and Children* (1861), *Smoke* (1867) and *Virgin Soil* (1876).

In Turgenev's novels one encounters again and again the effete gentry people, unable to cope with the task of adjusting themselves to the conditions and the age in which they live. The Childe Harold-Onegin-Pechorin tradition of the "superfluous man" therefore plays in them a conspicuous part. As early as 1851 Turgenev wrote his excellent *Diary of a Superfluous Man*, and from that time on this unheroic hero remained one of his ever-recurring figures. Rudin, his first full-size portrait in the novel bearing the same name, is actually one of Turgenev's amazing feats of characterisation.* We are introduced to Rudin in the drawing-room of an "up-to-date" country-house, where he impresses everybody by his intelligence and idealism (in the style of the 'thirties). Then, to our surprise we learn that this brilliant talker is a parasite and a sponger. Soon we are compelled to revise this opinion also. After a number of contradictory features quickly following one another, he is subjected to a crucial test—in his love for the hostess's daughter Natasha. But here he shows his lack of backbone and even of ordinary courage. The author makes us alternately waver between spite, pity and affection, and each new feature of Rudin perplexes us as if it could not belong to the man we know already. Yet after a while all the

* Rudin is supposed to be a portrait of the famous revolutionary Michael Bakunin, whom Turgenev knew well in his student days at Berlin.

contradictions adjust themselves, and we have before us an intensely real character whom, for all his strangeness, we seem to like. Full of the best impulses and intentions, but as helpless in practice as a child, this uprooted *déclassé* is unable to find an active contact with life. So he is doomed to remain a victim of his own dreams, and his brilliant intelligence remains sterile, however good the stuff out of which he is made.

If Rudin is a restless descendant of Onegin gone to seed, Natasha has affinities with Pushkin's Tatyana. Like Tatyana, she too is much stronger than the man she loves, and after her initial disappointment, finds her place in life. The whole existence of Rudin, however, is only one long series of escapes—from life as well as from himself. He embodies the woolly rootless idealism which was so often to be found among the gentry intellectuals of the 'forties, and it is almost with a kind of relief that we learn of his death on the barricades in Paris, during the Revolution in 1848.

The note of frustration is no less strong in Turgenev's next novel, *A Nest of Gentlefolk*. Here, too, we have a picture of gentry life against the background of which the Rudin-Natasha (i.e. Onegin-Tatyana) motif assumes, in the love between Lavretsky and Liza, a rather tragic turn. Lavretsky, a disillusioned married man whose lewd wife is enjoying herself on the French Riviera, is in essence as "superfluous" as Rudin but more purposeful. During his wife's absence he falls in love with a woman after his own heart (Liza) and, in spite of their mutual reticence, knows that his feelings are reciprocated. Suddenly Lavretsky reads in a newspaper that his wife has died. The situation is changed at once. The two lovers joyfully realise that now they can become man and wife. But here Mme Lavretsky unexpectedly turns up—the rumour of her death in France having been false. She actually comes back with the diplomatic intention of obtaining her husband's forgiveness. Unable to disentangle himself from the grip of his depraved legal wife, Lavretsky surrenders to his fate without a struggle, while Liza buries her own life in a convent. Here, after a considerable lapse of time, the two once happy lovers meet again in a scene which might have become melodramatic but for Turgenev's supreme artistic tact and restraint. For not a single word is exchanged, and the two pass each other by like two pathetic ghosts.

Delicate on account of its pitfalls, the subject-matter is worked out in a symphonic manner—with numerous secondary motifs, episodes and characters held together by the basic theme. The contrasted and mutually complementary characters ; the background, the "atmosphere" and the plot itself are so well blended that here the truth of life is not only distilled but also deepened and intensified by the truth of art. Even Turgenev's mood of gentle fatalism, which pervades the book, is so well sublimated as to cease to be personal : it becomes part and parcel of the "atmosphere" itself. And so does his admiration for Liza. She may be idealised, but this does not prevent her from being alive and real—a thing which can be said, perhaps, with less emphasis of Helena, the heroine of *On the Eve*.

In this novel Turgenev portrayed the generation of

the 'fifties, that is, of the years which saw the Crimean Campaign, the death of Nicholas I, and anticipated the great reforms that were to come during the next decade—the years of expectations. But were the Russian intellectuals equal to the tasks ahead? Turgenev's answer was in the negative—at least with regard to men if not to women. The heroine of this novel is represented (on the very eve of the Crimean Campaign) as the new active woman, capable of a heroic task without any heroic pose or self-admiration. Surrounded by charming and intelligently talkative Rudins, she falls in love not with a member of her own class or even her own nation, but with the rather angular Insarov—a Bulgarian fanatically devoted to the idea of freeing his country from the Turkish yoke. But if Helena remains convincing, Insarov is too overdrawn, too much of a one-track mind, to be entirely alive. One admires his firmness rather than his personality, but in the end it is his firmness again which makes one feel somewhat dismayed. It is worth noting that even this novel, in which Turgenev was so anxious to portray a strong man, has an unhappy ending: Insarov dies in Venice, while on his way to foment a rising in his own country.

It was only in his next and greatest novel, *Fathers and Children*, that Turgenev succeeded in giving a convincing portrait of the strong new man—this time a Russian—the age was clamouring for. And since he was doubtful of the members of his own class, he had to look for him among the "commoners." He found him in the person of the nihilist Bazarov, whose prototype was a Russian doctor Turgenev had actually met in 1860, in Germany. It was not without malice that he transferred Bazarov to a "nest of gentlefolk," confronting him with the rather fossilised representatives of the 'forties. Devoid of any respect for traditions, canonised ideas or class-distinctions, Bazarov is frankness itself—always matter-of-fact, inconsiderate, even aggressive, but at the same time hard-working and full of guts. One can well imagine that the role he plays in the genteel "Victorian" country-house of his hosts is none too pleasant for either party. Various conflicts, hidden and open arise almost at once, and they are caused not so much by the differences in views and opinions as by those imponderable unconscious attitudes towards certain things in life which are often a much more formidable class-barrier than rank or wealth. Turgenev surpasses himself in the fineness of touch and delicate humour when dealing with those imponderables. On the other hand, he may admire Bazarov, but does not really like him and feels more at home with the "gentlefolk." Yet he realises that the future is with Bazarov and not with Bazarov's hosts, whom the "nihilist"* cannot quite stomach. Bazarov was in fact the "commoner" who emerged among the leading figures in the intelligentsia of the 'sixties, and with whom the "gentlemen" had to put up whether they liked him or not. A "gentleman" himself, Turgenev gave in Bazarov one of the great portraits in the nineteenth century literature.

From a purely formal standpoint, *Fathers and*

* It was Turgenev who introduced the word "nihilist" into literature.

Children is as perfect as *A Nest of Gentlefolk*, but its texture is richer, while the interplay of the characters is considerably deeper. The "tame" Arkady (with whom Turgenev himself must have had quite a lot in common), Arkady's father and immaculate uncle, Bazarov's pathetically simple parents, the shy Fenitchka, the self-possessed (and undersexed) Mme Odintsova, her gentle sister Katya—they all fit perfectly into the pattern devised by the author and are alive even in their most casual words and movements. The finale is again a tragic one. Yet the scene of Bazarov's death is one of the most powerful ever described by an author—powerful precisely on account of its reserve. The contrast between Bazarov's manly stoicism and the frantic state of his parents—so anxious to conceal their despair from their dying son—is one of those marvels of art which are more real than reality itself. Although the novel is permeated with the atmosphere of the early 'sixties, it is easy to perceive behind it all the eternal tragi-comedy of human relations in general: those between parents and their grown up children; between men and women; aristocrats and "commoners"; dreamers and realists; leaders and followers. It is again a case of the truth of life being deepened and enriched by the truth of art.

IV

THE IMPATIENT YOUNGER GENERATION OF THE 'SIXTIES repudiated *Fathers and Children.* The storm raised by the novel brought so much disgust to its author that, for a while, he intended to give up literature altogether, as one can gather from his autobiographic sketch, *Enough* (1864).* Turgenev's irritation at the Russian life of the period came out with a great deal of bitterness also in his next novel, *Smoke*. As if feeling that he himself was now becoming more and more "superfluous," he preferred to live abroad where he counted among his friends some of the foremost literary figures of the day, including his great admirers George Sand, Gautier, Sainte-Beuve, Flaubert, Renan, the brothers Goncourt, Taine, Daudet, Zola and Maupassant. Yet life seemed to have lost its flavour, its contents and intensity—even its *negative* intensity—as far as he was concerned. "The most terrible thing is that there is nothing terrible in life ; that life's very essence is meanly-uninteresting and beggarly-flat." This brief saying of his—so much like Gogol's complaint about great Tedium—sums up his weariness and pessimism, both of which may have been a partial outcome of his infatuation for the famous singer Mme Viardot-Garcia. Turgenev had met her in his twenties, while at Petersburg, and that virile and in her own way brilliant woman remained his life-long love. Although, for some curious reason, their relationship seems to have been purely platonic,† the enamoured author followed her all over Europe and spent also his last years near her.

* This sketch was cruelly parodied by Dostoevsky (under the title, *Merci, Merci, Merci*) in *The Possessed*.

† One is inclined to suspect that Turgenev embodied some of Mme Garcia's features in the portrait of Mme Odintsova.

Because of these wanderings he must have felt the more sadly uprooted at times. Still, he was less out of touch with what was going on in Russia than many of his critics thought. Turgenev the artist may have been above parties, but as a citizen he was keenly interested in the political and social life of his country. Even after his differences with the "commoners" in *The Contemporary*, his outlook remained that of a liberal Westerner, for which the patriotic Slavophil Dostoevsky lampooned him (so mercilessly) in the figure of the author Karmazinov in *The Possessed*. The controversy between the two factions found an echo in *Smoke*—a novel in which biting personal indignation and political satire, directed against all the factions of Russian life, often loom large even at the expense of the finely worked out romance, or the unsuccessful renewal of an old romance, between Litvinov (another "superfluous man") and Irina. On the other hand, Turgenev the portrait painter achieves here one of his greatest triumphs with Irina—a more sparkling, more complex and subtly evasive personality than any of his previous heroines. Mr. Edward Garnett is right in defining her in his study of Turgenev as a woman with "that exact balance between good and evil which makes good women seem insipid beside her and bad women unnatural. She ardently desires to become nobler, to possess all that the ideal of love means for the heart of a woman ; but she has only the power given to her of enervating the man she loves. She is born to corrupt, yet never to be corrupted. She rises mistress of herself after the first measure of fatal delight. And, never giving her heart absolutely to her lover, she nevertheless remains ever to be desired. Further her wit, her scorn, her beauty, preserve her from all the influences of evil she does not deliberately employ. Such a woman is as old and as rare a type as Helen of Troy."

With all its occasional flaws, *Smoke* is one of Turgenev's masterpieces. His last novel, *Virgin Soil*, on the other hand, can more aptly be called a brilliant failure. Here the author obviously wanted to prove that, in spite of his stay abroad, he was able to understand and to interpret the aspirations of the advanced currents in his native country. In this case he tackled the current prevalent in the 'seventies—the "populism" which aimed at bridging the gap between the intelligentsia and the people and caused a number of enthusiastic youths and girls to sacrifice everything in order to help the masses and prepare them for the hoped-for revolution. In *Virgin Soil* we can follow the activities of a whole group of such enthusiasts up to their complete disappointment. Anxious to blend the social-political theme with the artistic side of the novel, the author nearly succeeded in it—nearly but not entirely. His weakness comes out first of all in the portrait of the principal character: the "strong man" Solomin. For instead of producing a new counterpart of Bazarov, Turgenev gave here something like an abstraction of a sober, reliable, practical idealist. Solomin is too much of a "perfect" dummy to be credible as a human being. The other characters of the novels are, however, convincing and alive: the actively generous Marianna (almost a twin-sister of Helena in *On the Eve*), for example ; the "superfluous" revolutionary Hamlet—Nezhdanov ; or the pompous opportunist (this time of a "liberal" brand) Sipyagin. The love between Nezhdanov and Marianna is, of course, a new variation of the Rudin-Natasha motif. The general tenor of the book is rather pessimistic about the populist movement, and Turgenev's own conclusions seem to tally with the allegorical poem by one of his heroes, *A Dream*, which contains the following not very hopeful lines:

> "*The Peasants sleep like the dead; they reap and plough asleep, they thresh*
> *And yet they sleep. Father, mother, all the family, all sleep.*
> *He who strikes sleeps, and he who receives the blow!*
> *Only the tavern is wakeful—and never closes its eyes;*
> *And clasping a whisky-pot with a firm grip,*
> *Her forehead at the Pole and her feet in the Caucasus,*
> *Sleeps a never-ending sleep our country, our holy Russia.*"

Turgenev described the various aspects of Russian life at a time when the sleeper, rubbing his eyes, was preparing to have his own say at last. What that say would be like remained a puzzle even for Turgenev. The solution of Russia's riddle and destiny lay in the future.

V

IN SPITE OF ALL THE CHANGES IN LITERARY FASHIONS, Turgenev still remains one of the greatest artists in

Russian as well as in European fiction. Apart from his mellow style, his polish, his delicate irony, and his sense of construction, one admires in him that indefinable intimacy with which he impresses his characters upon us even before we are aware of it. However strange they may appear at first, we soon move among them as among personal friends whose misfortunes often agitate us as much as our own. He excels in particular as psychologist and poet of love. And whatever theme or plot he may choose, he always knows how to treat it in the perspective of something deeper and more permanent than the passing show of a period. The variety of his characters, too, is surprisingly big. This is true also of his women portraits, despite his predilection for the Tatyana-type. Take the hysterically exalted girl in *A Strange Story* ; his gallery of old maids ; his worldly cocottes (Mme Lavretsky in *A Nest of Gentlefolk*, or Mme Polozova in the largely autobiographic *Spring Torrents*) ; his blue-stockings ; his enchantingly sensuous Irina in *Smoke*. Turgenev's weakness for Mme Viardot-Garcia may have been responsible for the large number of weak men in his novels and stories ; yet his weaklings are more interesting, more complex, and certainly more successfully worked out than his strong men. The futility of his own love is further reflected in his "atmosphere," reminiscent of a melancholy autumn afternoon, with gentle fatalism permeating the air.

The same kind of mood can be felt in his stories which are deservedly among the best in European literature. A master of impressionism in *A Sportsman's Sketches*, and a superb story-teller in such narratives as *First Love* (autobiographic), *Asya, A King Lear of the Steppes, The Spring Torrents*, and many others, he can stand comparison with any famous artist of the word. Most of his stories resemble well-organised reminiscences, told in the first person (his favourite device is that of setting a story within a story) and vibrating with that vague nostalgia for the past which was typical of Turgenev himself. As a "superfluous" member of an already "superfluous" class, he felt so homeless in the rapidly-changing world, that the atmosphere of doom eventually seemed to emanate from his very personality. Mme Herzen once compared him with an uninhabited room: "Its walls are damp, and their dampness gets into your bones ; you are afraid to sit down, afraid to touch anything, and you only wish to get out of it as quickly as possible."

Little wonder that disillusioned and tired as he was, he even had a few lapses from his high artistic level when, in *The Song of Triumphant Love* (1881) and *Clara Milich* (1882), he began to dabble in dilettantish spiritism and occultism. His exquisite *Poems in Prose* (known as *Senilia*) also reflect the weariness and the resignation of an old man who has nothing more to wait for than death. Turgenev the man died in 1883. But Turgenev the author continues to live—as a world classic, belonging not to one, but to all ages and countries.

SIX

Nekrasov

I

NEKRASOV'S POETIC ACTIVITIES COINCIDED WITH A TIME when the Pushkin tradition was already in the hands of epigones rather than original creators. Unwilling as well as unable to be an epigone, he eventually struck a new path of his own, the novelty of which can perhaps best be explained through his personality on the one hand, and the character of the age in which he lived on the other. Born in 1821, Nikolai Nekrasov matured with the generation of the 'forties—the period of the rise of the intelligentsia, but with a prevalence of the advanced gentry mentality in their midst. The "Decembrist" spirit was not yet dead, and there was a regular cult of the political martyrs still toiling in the mines of Siberia. Typical products of that spirit, grafted upon Hegel's philosophy, were such members of the gentry class as Herzen and Bakunin, both of whom contributed to the revolutionary thought of Europe. It was only in the 'sixties that the share of the "commoners" in the literary, cultural and political activities rapidly increased. But whereas the "gentlemen," relying on their estates, had enough leisure to write without worrying about their daily bread, most of the "commoners" lived from hand to mouth as journalists and pamphleteers. At times they were compelled to be purveyors of vaudevilles, hastily written *feuilletons*, topical doggerel and other commercialised genres.

Nekrasov, who belonged to both generations, had to do his literary apprenticeship towards the end of the 'thirties and in the early 'forties. It was a hard school and full of bitter experiences. The more so because his father, an officer and a landowner of the old brutal type, had left him without any support at the age of seventeen. He sent his boy from Yaroslavl on the Volga to Petersburg with the intention of making him an officer, but as the future poet refused to have anything to do with the Cadet Corps, he was at once deprived by his parent of financial help and left to his own devices. Starving and freezing in the streets of Petersburg, Nekrasov lived for a while the life of a down-and-out. Things were often so bad that he had to be sheltered by compassionate beggars in dosshouses. He never forgot the lessons learned during these trials, but he managed to get out of it comparatively soon. His first step towards something better consisted of journalistic hackwork. Prolific as he was in both verse and prose, he acquired already at this time a certain cheap facility and disregard for good taste, which stuck to him to the end —even during his best period. The ambition to succeed as a poet made him write a volume of "serious" verse, *Dreams and Sounds*, which he published in 1840. It was a collection of immature and derivative poems (with strong traces of Zhukovsky's influence), and the critic Belinsky attacked it so violently that the book had neither literary nor financial success. Undaunted, Nekrasov added to his functions those of an editor and publisher. He was introduced to Belinsky, and before long the two men were friends and fellow workers. At the beginning of 1846 he edited *Petersburg Miscellany*, with Turgenev's *Three Portraits* and Dostoevsky's first novel, *Poor Folk*, as its *pièces de résistance*. The success was enormous. In the same year he was able to acquire (together with Panayev) *The Contemporary* which he turned from a rather tame organ into a periodical of the revolutionary democracy in Russia. In addition to the best authors of the day, he succeeded in having among his contributors such radical "commoners" as Chernyshevsky and Dobrolyubov—the leading pamphleteers and critics during the 'sixties.

That decade had begun with the liberation of the serfs and other far-reaching reforms, but the unfortunate Polish rising of 1863-64 marred a number of hopes. The suppression of the Poles by Muravyov, nicknamed the "Hangman," was so brutal indeed that the Tsar himself, who was still under the influence of liberal advisers, felt disgusted and made no bones about it. Yet after the attempt on the Tsar's life (on April 4th, 1866) by Karakozov, the previously sacked

"Hangman" came into power once again, and this created considerable panic among the radicals. Nekrasov, known by then all over Russia as a poet and also as the editor of the most liberal periodical in the country, hoped to bribe Muravyov by writing some verses in his honour (which he himself recited at a banquet), but even such a shameful trick failed to work—*The Contemporary* was suspended forthwith. It was only two years later (1868) that Nekrasov managed to get hold of another important periodical, *The Fatherland's Annals*, which he edited with the help of Saltykov-Shchedrin (the author of *The Golovlyov Family* and the greatest Russian satirist of that period) and the sociologist Mikhailovsky. Under their joint guidance the periodical became the leading organ of the "populist" trend of thought. The strange thing, however, was that Nekrasov managed to combine his editorial and literary energy with all sorts of excesses which also required money. He gambled, hunted, entertained on a lavish scale, kept expensive cooks and even more expensive mistresses. In the end he became involved (together with his mistress Mme Panayeva) in a shabby financial transaction with regard to the entire fortune belonging to the feeble-minded wife of the expatriated poet Ogaryov—all this, while he was writing sincere, deeply-felt poems about the people's woe and injustice. But he was already afflicted with an incurable disease in his throat, which started in 1853 and lingered on until, on January 8th, 1878, he died. He was accompanied to his grave by the "populist" generation of the 'seventies which saw in Nekrasov, whatever his private character, their inspiring mouthpiece and a truly great poet.

II

AFTER HIS LACK OF SUCCESS IN 1840, NEKRASOV FOUND his own poetic voice rather late—towards the end of the 'fifties and in the first half of the 'sixties. As for the general trend of that poetry, it had a number of causes, some of them fairly complicated and going back to his experiences at home and in St. Petersburg. In boyhood he witnessed the cruel treatment meted out to the serfs, as well as to his mother (a Polish woman of some education and refinement), by his rough father. In Petersburg again he saw the very depth of misery bred by a modern city. His opposition to everything that was connected with serfdom and autocracy made him write civic poetry, whereas his sympathy with the oppressed serfs drove him towards the people and was responsible for the voice of a "repentant nobleman" in his work. To this the realism of his big city poems, dealing with the Petersburg he had learned to know, should be added. In one of them, beginning with the line, "When I drive at night in a darkened street," he describes, with haunting directness, a starving couple whose baby has died. Both of them have been reduced to such straits in their garret as to be unable to buy a coffin in which to bury their child. In the end the young and still pretty mother is compelled to go on the streets whence, after a while, she returns—her eyes full of despair and shame—with the money for the coffin. The extremes of such misery appealed to Nekrasov as much as they did to Dostoevsky, and he was among the first to add the big city motifs to Russian poetry. His *Street Scenes* and pictures of Petersburg outcasts were further enlarged by social satires, by caustic scenes from bureaucracy and high life, which border, however, on his civic poems proper. The bulk of his civic and political poetry can be dismissed as rhymed pamphleteering. If we want to find Nekrasov at his best and most original, we must look for him in the poems he wrote about the people or at least in the manner of the people.

Had Nekrasov relied upon a solid literary and poetic culture, he might perhaps have become a follower of the Pushkinian tradition at a time when the polished "Parnassian" school of Alexey Tolstoy, Apollon Maikov, Polonsky and Fet was in the ascendant. But he either had no wish or no time to acquire such culture. So he began to trust entirely his innate poetic feeling which came not from literary poetry but from the rhythmic and melodic patterns of the folk-song. All that is great in Nekrasov the poet came from this source. It was on this ground, too, that his sympathy and affinity with the people served him in good stead. Whatever one may think of his political, civic and didactic verses, there can be no doubt of the power and the melody he extracted from the folksong. He is one of the few instances of great individual poetry created as it were on the plane of the collective folk-genius.

Elements of such creative *rapprochement* with the people can be found before him—in Pushkin, Lermontov, and especially in Koltsov, but none of them went as far in this direction as Nekrasov. It may have been partly for this reason that the "populist" Chernyshevsky put Nekrasov higher than Pushkin and Lermontov.

Nekrasov's flair for the melody of the folksong (with its peculiar rhythms and verbal instrumentations) was certainly stronger than in any of the previous poets. It was he, moreover, who introduced and cultivated on a large scale the dactylic endings* typical of the *byliny* and of the Russian folksong in general. He came so near the genius of the people that some of his poems have been included in the folksongs and are now sung by the Russian masses from one end of the country to the other. Through his peculiar assimilation of the folk-style (especially his blend of anapaests and iambics with dactylic endings) he enlarged the scope and the area of Russian poetry, while building up a bridge between literature and the people. Having turned, on so many occasions, against the accepted canons, he made the next step and tried to "de-poetise" literary poetry by introducing all sorts of unpoetic "peasanty" words.† It is the genuine folk-flavour that makes a number of his poems (including *The Pedlars*, *The Green Rustle*, and the whole of his epic *Who is Happy and Free in Russia?*) untranslatable. For even the best

* They were used before him by Lermontov and Koltsov.

† This process of de-poetisation was equally strongly marked in his civic verses (addressed mostly to the "populist" intelligentsia) and abounding in words taken from ordinary journalism. It often became topical journalistic verse pure and simple.

rendering of the contents does not do justice to them as poems unless one catches all the peculiarities of Nekrasov's rhythm and melody, and these are inseparable from the Russian language. So much for Nekrasov's technique. Another strong point of his work is its village realism which also deserves to be dwelt upon.

III

NEKRASOV'S BIG CITY REALISM HAS ALREADY BEEN mentioned. It was partly connected with his civic poetry, and owed a great deal to the "natural school", sponsored by Belinsky. The same holds good of his poems directed against his own class—the poems of a "repentant nobleman" who, for moral as well as humanitarian reasons, became a defender of the peasant and the village. In this respect he followed in the footsteps of Pushkin's *In the Country*, whereas his best political verses can be linked to those of the executed "Decembrist" Ryleyev.* In some of his poems, such as *Meditation at a Porch*, *Song to Erémushka*, *A Knight for an Hour*, *The Railway*, all these motifs converge, imbued as they are with Nekrasov's own gloomy and aggressive moods. One of the typical examples is his *Home*.

* His unfinished series *Russian Women* (1872) was originally called *The Decembrist Wives*. The two sections completed deal with Princess Trubetskaya and Princess Volkonskaya, both of whom joined their husbands. The series is by no means among his best products.

It makes one think of Lermontov's indictments (but it is stronger) and of Pushkin's *In the Country*, with the difference that the "repentant nobleman" Nekrasov openly accuses himself, his own ancestors and particularly his own father. This is how it begins:

Behold it once again, the old familiar place,
Wherein my fathers passed their barren vacant days!
In muddy revels ran their lives, in witless bragging;
The swarm of shivering serfs in their oppression found
An enviable thing the master's meanest hound;
And here to see the light of heaven I was fated,
And here I learned to hate, and bear the thing I hated;
But all my hate I hid within my soul for shame,
And I at seasons too a yokel squire became;
And here it was my soul, untimely spoilt and tainted,
With blessed rest and peace too soon was disacquainted;
Unchildish trouble then, and premature desires,
Lay heavy on my heart, and scorched it with their fires.
Nay, from those younger years of harshness and rebelling
No recollection brings one comfortable ray.

Vividly remembering the sad lot of the serfs, he was never able to dissociate it from the sufferings of his own bullied mother, for whom he conceived—at least after her death—a regular cult, as one can conclude from the following lines in the same poem:

Here is the dark, dark close. See where the branches thicken,
What figure glimpses down the pathway, sad and stricken?
Too well the cause I know, my mother, of thy tears;
Too well I know who marred and wasted all thy years.

For ever doomed to serve a sullen churl untender,
Unto no hopeless hope thy spirit would surrender ;
To no rebellious dream thy timorous heart was stirred ;
*Thy lot, like any serf's, was borne without a word.**

In the end Nekrasov experiences something like moral satisfaction when seeing his ancestral home well nigh ruined. On the whole, the virulence of his indictment was always in direct ratio with his own repentance—that of an individual landowner and the representative of a class in one. Repentance, or rather a mood of ever-recurring moral masochism and self-castigation, may well have been needed by him even as a creative stimulus. This alone would be enough to throw some light on the duality of his behaviour during the years of his prosperity : on the one hand the sumptuous living typical of a former squire, and on the other his constant and sincere self-reproaches, turned into poetry. And the more he hated the remnants of the squire in him, the more acutely he felt also the people's tragedy and the people's cause, with which he was anxious to identify himself as a poet.

No other Russian intellectual has ever succeeded in coming so close to the simple folk and the village as Nekrasov did—at least during his "populist" moments. His realism of the countryside is often similar to that of George Crabbe, although he does not entirely concentrate on the negative and tragic side of village life. There are bright verses in it, too, especially those depicting the village urchins. What could be more delightful

* Translated by Oliver Elton in *A Book of Russian Verse* (Macmillan).

than the realism of his poem, *Peasant Children*, in which he describes a bevy of village boys, clandestinely looking at him through a cranny and making comments! Here is its beginning:

Again in the country! A life full of pleasure,
I shoot; I write verses in solitude deep;
And yesterday, searching the moorland for treasure,
I came to a cowshed, turned in, fell asleep.
I woke. Through a crack in the wall had come prying
The sun's joyous rays, in profusion of gold,
A pigeon is cooing; some young rooks are flying
Just over the roof, in a chorus they scold.
Another bird raises an outcry uncanny,
I think by its shadow a crow it must be,
But hark! There's a whisper! And lo, through the cranny
A row of bright eyes gaze intently at me.
Yes, grey, black and blue eyes in earnest reflection
*Are mingled together like flowers in a field.**

Equally delightful are his poems—humorous, descriptive, didactic—dedicated to Russian children: *Uncle Jack*, for instance; *General Toptygin*, in which the frightened peasants mistake a run-away bear for an angry General; or *Grandad Mazay*, who during a spring flood rescues a boatful of hares and would not touch the bewildered creatures, but releases them instead, though with a warning:

God speed you! Hurry
Straight to shelter.
But look, my friends,

* Translated by Juliet Hoskice in *Poems by Nekrasov* (O.U.P).

Though now I free you,
When summer ends
Don't let me see you :
I raise my gun—
*Your day is done!**

Not all his poems about the peasants and the village are written in this vein. In the majority the sad and gloomy disposition prevails. Nekrasov's verses about the people's woe always strike the right note and are particularly moving when he sings of the hard lot of the Russian peasant woman. The account in *Orina —a Soldier's Mother* of how an old woman's only son, a healthy young giant, had been forcibly conscripted and after a few years returned home a complete wreck only in order to die of tuberculosis, is heart-rending in its tone and simplicity. Then there are the suffering toilers on the Volga and elsewhere, whom the poet asks at the end of his famous *Meditation at a Porch*, whether the only thing they have given to the world is their "song resembling a groan," after which they are perhaps doomed to disappear. Nekrasov himself wavers in his answer, but not very long. For behind the tragedy of his people he feels also their strength, as well as that broad, generous goodness which only comes from strength. And his admiration for them is testified by a number of his best poems, such as *The Green Rustle*, *The Pedlars*, *Vlas*, *The Red-Nosed Frost*, and *Who is Happy and Free in Russia ?*

* Translated by Juliet Hoskice. Op. cit.

IV

THE FIRST OF THESE IS A LYRICAL DRAMA IN MINIATURE. The bracing rhythm of the opening verses (in which the dactylic endings prevail) is itself sufficient to suggest the arrival of spring. The manner, the accent and the imagery are those of the peasants. Even the blossoming trees sway as white as if someone had "poured milk over them." And then we listen to a peasant who, on his return home from Petersburg (where he had been working), learned that his wife had been unfaithful to him. All through the winter he had brooded resentfully, until in the end he sharpened a knife with which to kill her. Suddenly spring arrived and drove all evil intentions out of his mind. As though spell-bound, his heart could not resist the wave of generosity and forgiveness brought along by so much beauty. The final note of the poem is a conciliatory one:

Love as long as you can,
Suffer as long as you can,
Forgive as long as you can,
And God be your judge!

The Pedlars is a series of poems about the enterprising Yaroslav peasants, peddling their wares in the country-side:

Making profit with each mile;
Everything they chance to meet with
Serves the journey to beguile.

In this series Nekrasov came so near to the accent and the spirit of the people that its opening poem has actually become a folksong:

Oy! How full, how full my basket!
Calicoes, brocades, a stack,
Come, my sweeting, make it lighter,
Ease the doughty fellow's back.
Steal into the rye-fields yonder,
There till night-fall I'll delay,
When I see thy black eyes shining
*All my treasures I'll display.**

There follow the pedlars' jokes, arguments and adventures with the village fŏlk. As a contrast to their carefree gaiety the *Song of a Poor Pilgrim* is interpolated, the wailing words and rhythm of which can hardly be rendered in any other language but Russian.

I pass through the meadows—the wind in the meadows is moaning:
"Cold I am, pilgrim, cold I am.
Cold I am, dear one, cold I am."
I pass through the forest—the beasts in the forest are howling:
"We are hungry, oh, pilgrim, we're hungry!
Hungry, oh dear one, hungry!"

The whole of the unhappy, neglected and exploited peasant Russia is thus reviewed, and each line ends with the refrain of either "cold" or "hungry," the slow repetition of which in Russian (*hólodno, gólodno*) suggests the moaning of the wind or the howling of the

* Translated by Juliet Hoskice. Op. cit. The same applies to all quotations from Nekrasov, except the last one (at the end of V).

hungry beasts. The motif of desolation in this poem also prepares the reader for the tragic end of the cycle. For the two pedlars are murdered by a woodman who robs them of all their money and is, in his turn, arrested the same evening, while carousing in a village inn.

The poem *Vlas*, which was much admired by Dostoevsky (he wrote about it in *The Diary of an Author*), portrays a thoroughly Russian figure: a repentant sinner after the people's heart. He is a former village *kulak* who used to exploit without mercy friend and foe alike—

> *Snatched the bread from needy neighbours*
> *While, in famine's hideous reign,*
> *Not a coin would leave his pocket*
> *Unrepaid by threefold gain.*

But during a heavy illness he had a vision of hell, horrifying enough to make him repent of all his evil deeds and to become a new man. With the same firmness of purpose with which he formerly robbed his fellow-beings, he now gave up his earthly possessions and became an ascetic—

> *All his wealth in gifts bestowing,*
> *Destitute did Vlas remain.*
> *Wandered barefoot, homeless, begging*
> *Money for God's church to gain.*

Red-Nose Frost (1863) represents the peak of Nekrasov's poetry. Although written in conventional metres, it is a perfect blending of realism, peasant-mentality and folklore. The theme is simple. Prokel, the husband of young Darya, has died and, in severe wintry weather, is buried with all the peasant rites and customs. After the burial Darya returns to her cold cottage, and in order to make it warm for her tiny children, she drives her horse Savraska to the neighbouring wood. While she gathers logs, King Frost espies her, swoops down, and makes her fall asleep. Freezing to death amidst the gorgeous scenery of the winter forest, she dreams of all the best moments connected with her married life, her fields, her two children Grishouka (Gregory) and Masha (Mary). The following section of the poem is typical of Nekrasov's realism, applied to the more idyllic side of a peasant's life and work:

In sparkling white hoarfrost encrusted
To cold overpowering she yields,
She's dreaming of radiant summer :
Some rye is still left in the fields—

It's cut though ; relieved they are feeling,
The peasants are piling it high,
And she, in another allotment,
Is digging potatoes close by.

The grandmother too is there working,
And on a full sack at their feet
The pretty rogue Masha is sitting,
And clasping a carrot to eat.

The big, creaking wagon approaches,
Savraska is turning her head,
And close to the bright, golden burden
Comes Prokel with ponderous tread.

"God keep you! And where is Grishouka?"
The father inquires, passing by,
"Among the sweet peas," say the women,
"Grishouka, Grishouka!" they cry.

He looks at the heavens. "I'm thirsty,"
He says, "And it's late too, I think."
And Daryushka rises and hands him
Some kvass in a pitcher to drink.

And meanwhile Grishouka comes running.
With garlands of peas he is bound,
A living green bush one might fancy
Is skimming along o'er the ground.

He runs! Eh! . . . As swift as an arrow!
He's burning the grass in his flight!
Grishouka is black as a raven,
His little head only is white.

He's shrieking with joy. There's a circlet
Of peas round his neck, like a wheel.
He gives some to mother and granny,
And sister. He twists like an eel!

From mother the mite gets caresses,
From father a sly little pinch,
And meanwhile Savraska's not idle:
She's stretching her neck, inch by inch.

She's reached them, the peas, sweet and juicy!
She's chewing and licking her lips
And raising her mouth, soft and loving,
The ear of Grishouka she nips.

V

THERE STILL REMAINS NEKRASOV'S CENTRAL WORK, *Who Can be Happy and Free in Russia?* (1873-76)—an epic, quite unique of its kind and occupying in his writings a position similar to that of *Evgeny Onegin* in the work of Pushkin. If *Onegin* combines and completes as it were all the ingredients of Pushkin's poetry, *Who Can be Happy and Free in Russia?* shows all the principal features of Nekrasov the poet gathered as though in a focus. The epic aims at giving a picture of the whole of Russia after the abolition of serfdom in 1861 and is written throughout in the people's style and language. The loom on which it is woven is that of a folk tale, but this only gives the poet a pretext for displaying all the realism, indictment, satire, boisterous humour and also didactic "purpose," of which he is capable. Seven poor peasants meet on a high road and begin to argue as to who is happy and free in Russia. They go on arguing until they come to blows. Then a little peewit is captured by them. The mother-bird, seeing this, offers them as ransom a magical napkin which, at their bidding, will produce in a moment all the food they ask for. They agree to it. Provided with such an unexpected gift,

The peasants unloosen
Their waist belts and gather
Around the white napkin
To hold a great banquet.
In joy, they embrace
One another and promise

That never again
Will they beat one another
Without sound reflection,
But settle their quarrels
In reason and honour
As God has commanded ;
That nought shall persuade them
To turn their steps homewards
To kiss wives and children,
To see the old people,
Until they have settled
For once and forever
The subject of discord :
Till they have discovered
The man who, in Russia,
Is happy and free.

Their Odyssey begins. In the course of it they encounter all sorts of people, take part in a rowdy village fair, get acquainted with such remarkable and truly strong characters as Klim the Elder and the peasant woman Matryona—a worthy counterpart of Darya in *Red-Nose Frost.* Uneven as a whole, the epic contains wonderful descriptive and lyrical passages, including fine paraphrases of the folk-song—*The Song about the Two Infamous Sinners*, for example. The scenes at the village fair are grotesquely amusing. Both humour and satire are provided by the figure of the doddering, crazy landowner Obolt-Obolduyev who refuses to accept the reforms of 1861. His heirs, afraid of making him angry and thus forfeiting the expected fortune, have—through bribery—persuaded the peasants to behave, until his rapidly approaching death, as though they were still serfs, which they do with much amusement. The panorama of new Russia passes before us in a variety of scenes, and whatever her trials, she has enough vigour and vitality to overcome them all. So the epic, although unfinished, ends in a note of faith. A spirited youth, Grisha Dobrosklonov (evidently meant for the critic Dobrolyubov), from among the "commoners," sees in his poetic dreams what is in store for his country and his people—dreams which are enough to chase away despondence and pessimism from the reader's mind.

Then Grisha tried vainly
To sleep; but half dreaming
New songs he composed,
They grew brighter and stronger . . .
Our peasants would soon
Have been home from their travels
If they could have known
What was happening to Grisha.
With what exaltation
His bosom was burning;
What beautiful strains
In his ears began chiming;
How blissfully sang he
The wonderful anthem
Which tells of the freedom
And peace of the people.

Such was the apotheosis of Nekrasov's own "populism" in poetry at a time when this trend prevailed in the intelligentsia. Finally, some mention should also be made of his purely personal lyrics. The best of them can be divided into two parts: one dealing with the continuous wrangles he had with his mistress Mme Panayeva (the wife of his fellow-editor of *The Contemporary*), and the other consisting of the poignant and tragic poems he wrote during the last period of his illness. Nekrasov was not a pleasant person to live with. Moody and sullen, he often would not say a word for days; and as for loyalty, he was no more addicted to it than the flighty Mme Panayeva. The years during which they lived together were certainly not years of harmony. But Nekrasov tried to make up for it at the end of it all by addressing to his mistress these lines:

Goodbye! Forget the days of wane,
Dejection, bitterness and pain,
Forget the storms, forget the tears,
Forget the threats of jealous fears.
But the days when the sun of love
Uprising kissed us from above,
And bravely we went on our way—
*Bless and forget not one such day.**

As for Nekrasov's poems referring to the last phase or phases of his illness, it is enough to say that they are among those deservedly famous lyrics, in which his "Muse of grief and vengeance" received a final touch.

* Translated by M. Baring in *A Book of Russian Verse*. (Macmillan.)

VI

AND WHAT IS NEKRASOV'S PLACE IN LITERATURE? Turgenev once said that the Muse of poetry had never spent a night in Nekrasov's verse. With all respect for Turgenev's aesthetic sense, such a verdict no longer holds good. The interest in Nekrasov's poetry has lately increased more than in that of any other poet since Pushkin. And for good reasons. By turning against the accepted canons, Nekrasov opened up new possibilities with regard to both technique and contents. Through his nearness to folk-poetry and folk-genius he actually helped to bridge the gap between the people and literature. By introducing a number of "unpoetic" themes in a purposely de-poetised language, he divested his verses of all solemnity on the one hand and of the danger of "prettiness" on the other. As a result, his directness made him accessible to the wider circles of readers. Even his journalistic verses (which are not of a high quality) performed a useful task in so far as they awakened and kept alive the interest in poetry among those readers who otherwise had little mental equipment for literature.

This was the reason why Nekrasov found so many ardent admirers among the "commoners" whose cultural background was considerably smaller than that of the "gentlemen" in the Russian intelligentsia. One of his recent critics, K. Chukovsky, is therefore justified in saying that Nekrasov wrote for a new type of political and social *consciousness*. Anyway, his work served as perhaps the most important link between the intelligentsia and the masses.

Nekrasov failed to create a school of his own. Nevertheless, his attitude towards the village, the people and the folk-poetry acted as an inspiration for several poets who came from the people (the greatest of them being Sergey Esenin). His attempt at marrying civic poety to topical journalism may not have been a happy union, but it has had a strong following in Soviet Russia, where Mayakovsky recently made a series of further brave experiments of this kind. Also the technical devices of Nekrasov's work have drawn much attention of late. This proves that Nekrasov is again coming into his own. We may no longer think (as some of his contemporaries did) that he is "greater than Pushkin." Still, with all his faults and virtues, he occupies one of the very high places in the Russian Parnassus.

SEVEN

A Note on Tolstoy and Dostoevsky

I

WHEN, IN THE 'SIXTIES AND THE 'SEVENTIES OF THE last century, Russian fiction reached its peak, it became clear that even apart from the novelty of the material there were quite a few aspects in which it differed, or tended to differ, from European fiction as a whole. What must have astonished many a Western reader was the "spaciousness," the depth, and the frankness with which the Russian authors often tackled the very essence of man, as well as the fundamental problems of existence. From Gogol on, Russian literature was certainly anxious to go beyond mere entertainment or even "mere art." Besides, in a country where literature was the only realm in which one still could express—if not otherwise, then at least in "Æsop's language"—that freedom of mind and spirit which was banned from the ordinary walks of life, the authors were being looked upon not only as artists of the word, but also as guides and teachers. There was a natural tendency to combine fiction with moral, philosophic, religious, social and political tasks even at the risk of encroaching upon the aesthetic side of literature. That is why the Russian novels so often abound in thoughts and discussions with regard to all sorts of vital questions, while yet trying to remain novels in the best sense of this word.

It is at this point, however, that the line between a philosophic and a mere philosophising novel should be drawn. The two are different and, in spite of their frequent resemblance on the surface, can be poles apart. In a didactic philosophising novel the characters have no existence independent of the author, but serve above all as pegs for the author's own attitudes and ideas—leading as a rule to certain foregone conclusions. Ideas are stuck on the characters instead of being embodied in them. The characters thus resemble either cleverly manipulated marionettes or else cartoons, the figures of which may look very lively at times without being actually alive. Many a "philosophic" tale in the 18th century can serve as an illustration to this effect. A brilliant modern equivalent of the same didactic kind is Bernard Shaw's *A Black Girl in Search of God*, the pedigree of which goes at least as far back as Voltaire's *Candide*. A true philosophic novel, on the other hand, is one in which thoughts and ideas are embodied in the characters in such an organic way as to become part and parcel of their inner lives and destinies, no matter whether the author himself agrees with what they say or not.

As soon as he begins to pull the strings behind them, the game is spoilt, however cleverly he may try to conceal it.

The same applies, and perhaps more so, to dramatic works. There is a world of difference between a lively dramatisation of a public lecture, and a drama of thoughts and ideas clashing with each other on equal terms within the consciousness of the characters concerned. Even if the author has a pet idea among them, he must know how to make it win on its own merits and not because he himself happens to agree with it. All this is not new, yet it may be worth mentioning in connection with the difference between Shaw and Ibsen, for example ; or, to take a much more involved case, between Tolstoy the preacher and Dostoevsky the seeker.

II

A COMPARISON BETWEEN THESE TWO GREATEST REPRESENTatives of Russian fiction has become (since Merezhkovsky's days) somewhat trite, but there still remain quite a few aspects of their work which can be further explored by comparing some of their basic differences. Thus it does not take long to discover that Dostoevsky can make his characters independent of himself even when using them as mouthpieces of his own views and tendencies—a thing which cannot be said to the same extent of Tolstoy after *Anna Karenina*. More than any other author, Tolstoy knows how to project into his characters all that touches upon the instinctive and physical side of man. Here he goes to the very root of life with that psychological as well as artistic integrity which can still amaze even the most exacting reader. But as soon as it comes to expressing views or ideas, a philosophy of life instead of life, Tolstoy shows his weakness. Far from making his characters independent of himself, he uses them as vehicles for his own views to the extent of endangering even their psychological probability.

This may not be so apparent in his earlier narratives, where "ideology" and psychology were considerably less differentiated than in his didactic writings after 1880, i.e. after his so-called conversion.

But even in Tolstoy's early writings one can detect his favourite method of showing in a parallel manner the various sides of one and the same theme in such a way as to leave one in no doubt as to which of them is preferable, without however forcing the intended issue. His story, *Three Deaths*, is an example. It consists of three parallel pictures of death, each of them practically independent of the other, but differing in the amount of the physical and moral torment involved. In the end it is quite clear what kind of death, and on what conditions, is least painful. The reader's conclusion is of course expected to coincide with that of Tolstoy's, even though it may not be unduly insisted upon by the author himself. The short novel, *Family Happiness*, gives us a parallel analysis of a young woman's love before and after her marriage to a much older husband. And again the reader is led to decide "independently" why non-sexual motherly love is preferable to the more passionate love in the first part of the novel. In *War and Peace* there are a number of themes, developing parallel with each other, or else intertwining as in a symphony, but for our purpose a comparison between the two principal seekers in the novel, Prince Andrey and Pierre Bezukhov, is of importance. Both of them represent the two contending doubles in Tolstoy's own personality ; yet he knew how to integrate, as far as possible, their quest with their total inner life and make it psychologically convincing.* He coped with the same dilemma, though less objectively, when dealing with the torments of Levin in *Anna Karenina*. The antagonism between "ideology" and psychology which came to a head after 1880, is here clearly anticipated.

As man and artist Tolstoy was one of the most full-blooded and "instinctive" human beings imaginable. While depicting the experiences on this plane, he was frankness and truth itself. Yet at the back of it all his moral consciousness kept watching, censoring and twisting, until at last Tolstoy was on the defensive against his own instincts, which he began to disparage so vehemently precisely because he was afraid of them. Having discovered a plausible ally in his rationalistic double, Tolstoy the moralist came to be at loggerheads with Tolstoy the man, and was anxious to force certain reasoned-out moral truths

* At the same time, the whole of his reasoned out anti-individualistic philosophy of history is interpolated as something which could be left out without any harm to the novel itself. In fact, the novel would be improved.

and ideas even when these were stressed at the expense of psychology and of the truth of life. So he was bound to be in conflict with Tolstoy the artist as well, since the excellence of art demands that even one's most personal ideas should be treated with the same aesthetic detachment as are those of any other characters in a novel or a play. Having reduced the meaning of life only to its *moral* meaning in the sense of the "improved" Sermon on the Mount, Tolstoy, who once had known and enjoyed the throbbing fullness of existence in all its aspects, eventually postulated in his writings that life itself—his own and everybody else's—be sacrificed to what *he* considered the meaning of life. According to him, the variety and broadness of human existence ought to be clipped down to his five virtuous rules even if all our cultural and technical achievements were doomed to perish forthwith. Some of his later works are blatant examples of how destructive all absolutist and abstract morality of this type can become, especially when divorced from life, history and culture. Sooner or later it identifies culture itself with immorality and turns against it as was the case with Tolstoy's idol Jean Jacques Rousseau and with Tolstoy himself.

III

THE HIDDEN CONTEST BETWEEN LIFE AND THE NARROWED down meaning of life led to some interesting contradictions even in Tolstoy's earlier works where he often turned, in spite of himself, against his own didactic moralism. But later on the moralist in him began to interfere, more and more, with Tolstoy the psychologist and the artist. In such works as *The Death of Ivan Ilyich*, *Master and Man*, and even *The Power of Darkness*, Tolstoy's genius succeeded in balancing the two antagonists—probably by means of an incredible *tour de force*. His preaching double asserted himself, however, rather disturbingly in a number of his other writings, including the well-known *Kreutzer Sonata* and *Resurrection*. Both works are powerfully written—after all Tolstoy was Tolstoy. Still, no one can pretend that Nekhlyudov, the "converted" hero of his last big novel, *Resurrection*, is convincing either as a convert or as a preacher. However excellent the other portraits and descriptions may be, Nekhlyudov remains a dummy. His "Christian" (i.e. Tolstoyan) teaching and preaching is so obviously pasted upon him by the author that in the end he bores us as he did the ex-prostitute Katyusha Maslova whose soul he was so anxious to "save" (not for her sake, of course, but in order to allay his own former guilt towards her and thus regain a peaceful conscience). One is not surprised that Maslova, after her contact with the political convicts, instinctively began to seek for something like a new life in the warmer and more charitable sphere of the revolutionaries who must have seemed to her a relief from Nekhlyudov's principled, cut-and-dried morality. In this way Tolstoy the psychologist turned again, inadvertently as it were and in spite of the author's intention, against Tolstoy the preacher.

Unable to sublimate his one-sided but unusually strong puritanical tendencies through his art, Tolstoy was bound to be tossed between the two even after he had rejected all art (including his own) which could not be stated in terms of morals. At bottom Tolstoy the preacher was much too dogmatic and deliberately one-sided to be a true seeker. What he wanted was inner safety rather than the kind of quest in which everything—morality included—becomes unsafe and problematic. If we want to see the drama of this quest in all its intensity, we can find it in the novels of the less puritanical and at the same time amazingly profound Dostoevsky.

IV

DOSTOEVSKY'S INNER STRUGGLE WAS HARDLY LESS PAINFUL than that of Tolstoy, but the antinomies he tried to cope with took place entirely in the realm of the spirit. And since he was in danger of becoming a victim of his own spiritual chaos, he had to clarify that chaos simply in order not to collapse underneath its weight. Hence the cathartic nature of his literary work. Endowed with a strong religious temperament, he was also a sceptic, a doubter, even a hidden nihilist who refused to take anything for granted. And this was not the only contradiction from which he suffered. Hence his quest. His very psychology was primarily a search for that ground on which he hoped to integrate the diverging elements of his split personality and to arrive at some tenable "leading idea" and affirmation of life. It was mainly for this reason that he explored the farthest realms of the Unconscious, of the human psyche, the processes and the findings of which he recorded in terms of art.

It needed Dostoevsky's creative genius to embody all the complications of such a quest in a series of novels —the most dramatic novels in European fiction. This explains the texture of his language, his style, his feverish pace (so different from the leisurely tempo of Tolstoy's great epics, *War and Peace* and *Anna Karenina*). His writings are as agitated as those of Gogol, but their diapason is wider and also deeper. What its compass could be like is clearly brought out by the inner conflict of Ivan Karamazov, a study of which alone is enough to show all the difference between Tolstoy's and Dostoevsky's methods.

Here we are indeed at the opposite pole of the self-sure preacher Nekhlyudov, and this applies to all the seekers in Dostoevsky's novels. Unlike those authors who use their characters as mouthpieces of their own pet ideas and sermons, Dostoevsky knew how to make thoughts and ideas spring from the innermost consciousness of his heroes. In doing this, he gave an equal chance to all the antagonistic "truths" by turning philosophy itself into a dynamic aspect of "psychology"—where thoughts were not reasoned-out precepts, but the stuff out of which human destinies are shaped.

Beginning with his *Memoirs of the Underworld*, Dostoevsky kept deepening this method in *Crime and*

Punishment, *The Idiot*, *The Possessed*, and *The Brothers Karamazov* in a manner which allowed an independent existence even to the characters voicing his most personal thoughts, sympathies and antipathies. That is why, in addition to being the greatest psychologist in modern fiction, Dostoevsky can be considered the creator of a new type of philosophic novel—as distinct from that didactic narrative which became the pitfall of Tolstoy's genius.

V

TO DRAW A FINAL COMPARISON BETWEEN THE TWO, THE longing of Tolstoy was turned back to a moralised and utterly static patriarchal past which, if it were possible at all, would amount to a denial of personality, of history and civilisation.* Dostoevsky's gaze, however, was anxiously as well as warningly directed to a future in which his intuition caught not only a number of disturbing possibilities about man's inner world, but also glimpses concerning such problems as Russia and Europe, the "decline of the West" (long before Spengler), the ultimate nature of Revolution, and particularly the calamitous results of our much too rapid scientific and technical progress—developing at the expense of an adequate moral growth. He foretold moreover the possibility of civilised cannibalism : of the

* Further aspects of this problem are dealt with in my book, *Tolstoy* (Methuen).

kind that has been practised *en gros* in the death-factories of Auschwitz and Belsen as a matter of daily routine and according to the last word of science. In *The Possessed* he showed man's appalling disintegration due to a loss of all inner values. In Ivan's *Legend of the Grand Inquisitor* he conjured up the vision of an even more appalling totalitarian humanity. And if ever there was a prophet of our recent apocalyptic catastrophes, such a prophet was Dostoevsky.

Like Alexander Herzen before him, Dostoevsky was horrified by the mean and irresponsibly philistine materialism of our European bourgeoisie. In spite of that, his attitude towards Western Europe was prompted not by hatred but by a sincere hope that Russia and the West would eventually join hands for the sake of a better and more dignified future. Aware of the fact that mankind would have to unite or else to perish, he aimed at a unity in the name of the highest religious and cultural values—such values in short as would change not only our jaded political and economic systems, but the very consciousness of the present-day man.

Such are some of the conclusions derived from Dostoevsky's quest as embodied in his principal novels. If Tolstoy eventually endangered his genius by trying to turn art itself into tendentious preaching, Dostoevsky as a rule expressed even his "philosophy" and occasional preaching in terms of art. And this only enhances the value of his novels of which it can truly be said that they have added a new dimension to Russian, as well as to European fiction as a whole.

EIGHT

Nikolai Leskov

I

RUSSIAN REALISM UP TO CHEKHOV IS KNOWN ABROAD mainly through the works of Turgenev, Goncharov, Dostoevsky and Tolstoy. But important though they be, these authors do not exhaust either the width or the pattern of that prodigiously creative period. One of its major representatives, Alexey Pisemsky, for instance, is hardly a name outside the boundaries of his own country, despite the fact that his novel, *A Thousand Souls* (1858), still ranks as a masterpiece in Russia. Equally unknown to the Western readers is the outstanding "populist" Gleb Uspensky. The same was the case, until quite recently, with Nikolai Leskov (1831-95) whose work is now finding, slowly but surely, due appreciation abroad, while at home his reputation stands very high indeed. No less a person than Maxim Gorky said of him (in the preface to one of Leskov's stories) that as a literary artist, Leskov can beyond any doubt be placed on a level with such masters of Russian literature as Tolstoy, Gogol, Turgenev and Goncharov. In its beauty and power, Leskov's talent is in no way inferior to theirs, and what is more—in his broad variety of themes he even surpasses any of his great contemporaries. His knowledge of Russian speech is supreme ; so is his gift of narrative for its own sake, not to mention his understanding of human beings. He may and does shape his characters by an artistic method different from, say, that of Tolstoy. On the other hand, he makes them speak for themselves in such a way that in the end they are as true, as convincing and even physically tangible as the characters created by his more famous contemporaries. Gorky further refers to him as the "most truly Russian of all the Russian writers" and "entirely free from outside influence."

A younger contemporary of the great realists, Leskov occupies a place of his own in Russian fiction, which, broadly speaking, developed along two main paths : one of them following the lucid simplicity of Pushkin, while the other preferred the somewhat overcharged style of Gogol. But Leskov's work fits into neither of these two categories. He stands by himself, and this fact can perhaps be explained partly by his origin and partly by the peculiar conditions which contributed to the development of his talent. Whereas practically all the old leaders of Russian realism came from the gentry, Leskov was of mixed origin, counting among his ancestors priests, traders and minor officials. This may have something to do with the wide range of his themes, with his lack of any social bias, as well as with his general approach to life. Socially he stood nearest to those "commoners" who came into their own in the active 'sixties. On the other hand, Leskov was much too independent, both as man and artist, to be pigeon-holed into any group or doctrine. Least of all was he inclined to indulge in the enthusiastic but often somewhat adolescent radicalism of the 'sixties, and openly defended religion at a time when "scientific" materialism was considered the hall-mark of fashion.

The same independence was shown by Leskov in his style, in his choice of the subject-matter, even in his attitude towards the accepted literary language. For, not unlike Nekrasov in poetry, it was he in particular who broadened Russian prose (hitherto based on the speech of the gentry) by grafting upon it the pattern and the inflection of the people's speech at its best. No author of his period was endowed with so strong a flair for the living spoken word as he. The word as such was something more than just a means to him—it assumed a value of its own, which he learned to feel and to appreciate mainly through his contact with simple folk. He also enlarged the area of Russian literature by introducing a great variety of new themes—some of them new enough to confound the contemporary critics and to defer his fame, making it posthumous. This had, however, a certain advantage : retarded fame is taken as a rule more seriously than that which comes too soon. But these facts become clearer only if his work is shown in conjunction with the man himself.

II

BORN IN THE TOWN OF OREL, THE ENVIRONS OF WHICH were made famous by Turgenev (in his *A Sportsman's Sketches*), Leskov breathed from his childhood the atmosphere of that provincial Russia which later became so inseparable from his writings. While still at the Grammar School, he witnessed the loss of the family fortunes—a blow which compelled him to interrupt his education and fall back upon his own resources. Full of vitality and common sense, he went into the world with courage, and had no reason for regretting it. Eventually he worked in Kiev, in the 'fifties, under a Briton—a certain Mr. Scott, the manager of the vast estates belonging to the Perovsky and the Naryshkin families. In the capacity of Mr Scott's agent, Leskov travelled all over Russia, and especially in the Volga provinces, thus widening his own experiences, his knowledge of the people and of the world. It was his British chief who, moreover, discovered in him a potential author and urged him to write. Having made his debut in 1860 (when he was nearly thirty years old), Leskov soon gave all his energies to literature and settled down in Petersburg, where he wrote for several periodicals, including

Dostoevsky's *Vremya* (Time), the peculiar populism of which must have been after his own heart.

It should be borne in mind that the 'sixties were a period of wrangles between political groups, notably between the conservative Slavophils on the one hand, and the liberal intellectuals of the "Western" orientation on the other. But whatever the differences among them, the fact remained that the intelligentsia as a whole had hardly any real contact with, or understanding for, the peasant masses. It was above all Dostoevsky who saw, or foresaw, the deeper implications of such a state of things and never wearied of pointing out that Russian intellectuals had no roots either in the soil or in the people of their native land. Hence his call for a deeper organic rootedness in both —a call which was endorsed by the poet and critic Apollon Grigoryev in his essays, by Alexander Ostrovsky in drama, and by Leskov in fiction. Incidentally, Grigoryev was one of the first critics to welcome Leskov's talent, which blossomed out in the second half of the 'sixties and continued to enrich Russian literature for a period of over thirty years. During that time Leskov wrote a vast amount of works which can be roughly divided into novels, chronicles of provincial life, stories pure and simple, semi-didactic legends, apocrypha, and lastly the so-called *skaz*—a sort of narrative connected mainly with his name and technically more important than any other facet of his work.

Leskov's two bulky novels, *The Impasse* (*Nékuda*) nd *At Daggers Drawn* (*Na nozhákh*), are political and touch upon the problems the generation of the 'sixties was called to face and to cope with. The first of them—it appeared in 1864—can be looked upon as an attempt on the part of the author to clear up his own attitude with regard to the extreme radical currents among the younger intelligentsia of the period. For this reason it is often included, though less so than *At Daggers Drawn*, in the series of novels comprising Turgenev's *Fathers and Children*, Goncharov's *The Precipice*, Pisemsky's *The Troubled Sea*, and Dostoevsky's *The Possessed*. As it happened, two years before the publication of his first novel, Leskov had written an article about a number of mysterious conflagrations in Petersburg, generally ascribed to the activities of the "nihilist" section among the students. Although written in defence of the students, the article was misinterpreted by the radical press which all at once discovered in Leskov an ideological enemy and raised a hullabaloo against him. In spite of his liberal tendencies and opinions, the author was thus willy-nilly driven into the opposite direction, and this made him adopt, in his very first novel, an aggressive attitude towards his accusers. But even *The Impasse* was a diagnosis rather than a direct attack. Leskov did not conceal in it his sympathy with the true and sincere idealists among the revolutionaries, while condemning without mercy the frauds, the fools, and the opportunistic camp-followers of radicalism. Like Dostoevsky in *The Possessed*, he saw in the extreme left section of the intelligentsia an uprooted and purely destructive element, unable to grasp either the real needs or the real tasks of Russia after the abolition of serfdom. It is a pity that he cheapened the plot by showing the revolutionaries as the dupes of Polish Jesuits in disguise, supposedly preparing the ground for the rebellion in Poland (in 1863) by fomenting internal troubles in Russia.

Vivid and full of incident, this work yet does not go beyond the average novels of the period. It falls infinitely below the level of such an apocalyptic book as *The Possessed.* So the hue and cry it caused among the radicals was quite out of proportion to its actual merit. As a result Leskov was, from now on, either ignored or else slandered by the radical press. Such a situation made him adopt an even more aggressive attitude towards his opponents, and he gave vent to it in his second political novel, *At Daggers Drawn* (1871), after which a reconciliation was out of the question. Still, it is worth mentioning that he never took part in any reactionary activities and was as outspoken about the excesses on the right as he was about those on the left. In a number of his writings he attacked the bureaucracy of the State and of the Church with such virulence as to risk—in 1883 for example—an open conflict with the authorities, while in 1889 one of his works was actually confiscated by the police on account of its "harmful" tendency.

Some of Leskov's earlier writings could conveniently be left out but for the fact that they point to certain questions of nineteenth century Russia—questions which transcend mere politics. The already mentioned "accursed problem" of the relationship between the intelligentsia and the people was one of them. Then there was the problem of individual adjustment during the economic and social changes after 1861 ; the problem of the *déclassé* from among the gentry, which made the once romantic "superfluous man" a topical character of Russian realism. Leskov himself—a rooted Russian if ever there was one—broached the theme of the "superfluous man" in his short novel *The Ones Passed-by*, and, very originally, in *The Islanders*, the hero of which is a gifted but unaccountable Russian artist, shown against the background of the ultra-respectable German settlers in Petersburg, whose milieu produced uprootedness of its own (illustrated by the heroine of the novel).

Leskov would probably have continued to write in the same vein, had he not come to the conclusion that after the hostile reception of his two political novels his literary future lay not in the novel at all. So he was on the look-out for a new genre, as one can gather from his next two works, *Cathedral Folk* and *The Sealed Angel*.

III

IN SPITE OF ITS LENGTH, *Cathedral Folk* (1872) IS NOT A novel in the usual sense of this word, but a bracing chronicle of life in a Russian cathedral town—with the clergy as the central characters. It was through this work that Leskov introduced the clergy into Russian literature as a new thematic element with such competence as to have added the two principal figures described, the archpriest Tuberozov and his helper Akhilla, to the memorable characters in Russian fiction. The contrast between the dignified, active idealist Tuberozov and the impulsive Akhilla (a typical Cossack who by some mistake joined the Church but could never quite fit into his profession) abounds in comic as well as pathetic incident. Akhilla worships his superior with the unquestioning admiration of a child and behaves like a jealous woman whose love, appreciated though it be, is studiously ignored. The amusingly colourful account of events is obscured by Tuberozov's troubles with the Church bureaucracy and ends in a sad note—the death of the archpriest and, not long after him, of the turbulent Akhilla, too.

The whole of this narrative is so admirably interwoven with the life of a provincial town and the surrounding district that some of its passages (the storm in the forest, for example) are among the gems of Russian prose. With the same success are rendered the peculiarities of the archaic speech used by the clergy. But while showing the vanishing patriarchal life in a sympathetic light, Leskov lays bare, and most scathingly, the dry, pedantic opportunism of the higher Church authorities. With even greater relish he caricatures the antics of the unscrupulous or frankly stupid sham-radicals and the would-be "new men" of the 'sixties.

But since *Cathedral Folk* is referred to as a chronicle and not as a novel, it is essential to stress the difference between the two, although they may overlap—in *War and Peace*, for example. Briefly, a novel is based on a plot the pattern of which is decisive for its structure. A "chronicle," on the other hand, is a sequence of incidents and happenings which occur as they do in real life. They may concern the same set of people, the same town or region, but the structure of the narrative is more loose than in a novel, and single incidents can often be added or else deleted without impairing the whole. In 1875 Leskov wrote about the "artificial and unnatural form of the novel" and pointed out the fact that in life things happen differently. "A man's life is like the unfurling of a scroll, and I am going to use the same method." He was as good as his word. He, moreover, endowed each of his characters with a voice and intonation corresponding to his profession and social position. This again led him to the *skaz*—a story usually told by a man of the people or by a lower middle-class person, with all the idioms, inflections and popular etymologies typical of the narrator himself. At the same time, Leskov took good care to render the traits of his characters not by means of analysis or by plastic descriptions, but by an accumulation of typical incidents and anecdotes. This method brought him, in its turn, close to the picaresque story which he dexterously combined with the *skaz*.

Less than a year after *Cathedral Folk* another of Leskov's masterpieces, *The Sealed Angel*, appeared. This is one of his finest and alas ! least translatable works. It combines in a striking manner his innate religious sense with the so-called *skaz* and is told by an artisan from among the dissenters or "Old-Believers" (the most patriarchal and staunchly religious portion of the Russian people) with that admirable use of the people's words and phrasing the flavour, or rather the stylisation, of which became, at the beginning of this century, something of a test for one's verbal art. While keeping to the chronicle-pattern in some of his other works, notably in the longish narrative *A Decayed Family* (1875), Leskov preserved the *skaz* and gave full scope to its form in such bracing stories as *The Enchanted Wanderer*, *A Tough Amazon* (*Voitelnitsa*), *The Steel Flea*, and *The Hare Chase.* The first of these is a picaresque tale of adventures told by an ordinary Russian who, after years of roaming, is about to become a monk and shares his reminiscences with a few pilgrims. The story is not only an illustration of the vitality and stoicism of the character concerned, but also of Leskov's skill in narratives of this kind. Some of the scenes, such as the dance of the gipsy belle whose tragedy is interwoven with the story, are described with an intensity of vision and of feeling which takes one's breath away.

A Tough Amazon is another *skaz*. It is told by a lower middle-class match-maker who, in the broadness of her character, becomes a procuress, and yet in spite of this preserves so much warmth and generosity in her simple heart that in the end one cannot help liking her. The hero of the hilarious *Steel Flea* is a left-handed smith from Tula whose sagacity outstrips even the inventive genius of England, but as was so frequently the case in old Russia—to no constructive or practical purpose. This *skaz* (perhaps the best known specimen of its kind) also reflects what might be called the instinctive attitude of Russian masses towards the English—an attitude of benevolence and admiration, but hardly devoid of the spirit of rivalry. The story itself was suggested to Leskov by the popular Russian saying: "The English made a flea of steel, but our artisans of Tula shoed it." As for *The Hare Chase*, first published in 1917, it is a life-story told, in the inimitably comic mixture of Russian and Ukrainian, by an upstart who came to grief. Devoid of brains and of scruples, but full of "zeal" for the powers-that-be, he wormed his way into the position of a police officer. Eventually he ruined both his career and his reason through having failed to catch a dangerous revolutionary who, during all that time, had been employed—cleverly disguised—as his coachman. *The Hare Chase* sparkles with fun and also with that satirical spirit which marked Leskov's writings in the 'eighties and the 'nineties, often bringing him close to Saltykov-Shchedrin—the Russian Swift of those days.

IV

EVEN IF LESKOV WAS NOT THE ACTUAL INVENTOR OF the *skaz* (the beginnings of which go back to Gogol and Pushkin), he nevertheless became its first undisputed master and brought it to such perfection as to secure for it a high place in Russian fiction. But he can be equally relied upon in the straightforward traditional story to which he added certain features of his own, such as an exciting plot and a quick and vivid action. A good example of this kind is his *Lady Macbeth of the Mtsensk District* (1865).* Taken from the *milieu* of the old-fashioned provincial merchants, it depicts the blind elemental passion—an obsession rather than passion—and the crimes resulting from it, with brutal yet powerful directness. The colours are plain, and the inner logic of crime and the punishment that follows is as inexorable as is the sway of carnal lust—the cause of it all. Needless to say, Leskov made even here splendid use of the people's language which, for all its realism, he often stylised in the manner of the chap-books of that period. It is one of Leskov's early stories, showing his ability to make characters alive exclusively in terms of incident.

This method can be studied in a number of his other narratives, especially those in which he keeps to the *skaz* type. The whole of *A Tough Amazon*, for example, is but a string of incidents and anecdotes arranged in such a manner as to make the woman convincing and real—as real in fact as if we had known her for years. The same can be said of *The Enchanted Wanderer*, or of *An Iron Will*—with its humorously-ironical portraiture of a German engineer in Russia. Leskov's experience of life was so rich indeed that quite a few of his jottings were left in the state of raw

* The Soviet composer Shostakovich made use of this story for his well-known opera under the same title.

anecdotic and semi-documentary reportage. Nor did he mind using the actual names of the people, historical or otherwise, who had taken part in the happenings recorded. *Cheramour*, Leskov's lower middle-class counterpart of Turgenev's *Rudin*, is an instance. So is *The Immortal Golovan* based, like *Cheramour*, on his reminiscences of a real person, the memory of whom still lingered in Leskov's native city of Orel. To this category can be added *On the Edge of the World*: an account of the hair-raising experiences of a Russian bishop (the Bishop of Yaroslavl) whose life was saved, during one of his diocesan journeys in the Arctic wastes of Siberia, by the loyalty and devotion of a pagan, while a Christian convert of the same tribe behaved like a cad. But since the implications of this story point to another group of Leskov's work, we can pass to those of his narratives which touch upon religious and ethical problems.

V

IT IS KNOWN THAT IN THE 'EIGHTIES LESKOV BECAME temporarily interested in Tolstoy and Tolstoyanism. Tolstoy, in his turn, commended the essential "Russianness" of Leskov and thus helped, as far as possible, towards his literary rehabilitation. For all that the gospel of the much-too-conscious self-perfection on the part of "converted" Tolstoy was unlikely to appeal, in the long run, to Leskov, whose Christianity (based on spontaneous warmth and goodness rather than on parading one's contrition, or the white robes of one's moral purity) was nearer to the people than that of Tolstoy. This attitude found an expression in his parables and legends—some of them paraphrased from the old Church-Slavonic *Prologue*, while others were taken from the folklore, or else from the general stock of the East-European Christian tradition. Such legends as *The Juggler Pamphalon*, *The Mountain*, *The Fair Azra*, deal with the early Christian period in Alexandria, but they lay stress on charity in Leskov's sense rather than on morality in the exacting sense of Tolstoy.

In Tolstoy the moral element was so much stronger than his religious consciousness that it actually throve at the latter's expense. Instead of integrating, it only further divided his incredibly rich personality by increasing the gap between Tolstoy the man and Tolstoy the moralist. This gap he tried to cope with by turning his reasoned-out puritanism into a new Categorical Imperative, that is, into a universally obligatory straitjacket in which there was more severity than genuine charity and love. Leskov, on the other hand, was endowed with a religious instinct spontaneous and powerful enough to save him not only from lack of charity, but also from conscious or unconscious moral exhibitionism—the two pitfalls of many a frowning puritan. If Leskov's art harbours a "message" at all, to which our (or any other) period might listen with profit, it is the simple truth that the thing most needful is human warmth and sympathy—as a preliminary condition of everything that makes life worth while. Leskov himself was richly endowed with this virtue. In his attitude towards the world there was nothing reminding one either of Gogol's rancour and distrust, or of Tolstoy's severe moral book-keeping. On the contrary, he found life attractive precisely because he approached it in the spirit of broadness, tolerance and charity. This explains why he was one of the few Russian realists able to depict also good characters convincingly—without any stilts, rhetorics and sermons. One of such characters is Tuberozov in *Cathedral Folk*. But we can find plenty of them in his other works too—in *The Musk-Ox*, *Kotin and Platonida*, *Cheramour*, *The Immortal Golovan*, etc., which only enhances his place in literature.

VI

THE RANGE OF LESKOV'S TALENT IS FURTHER ILLUSTRATED by the wealth of his motifs and genres. Novels, naturalistic stories, *skaz*-tales, legendary and folk-lore themes, anecdotic reminiscences, intensely documentary pictures of the serfdom period (*The Beast*, *The Make-up Artist*, *The Vale of Tears*, etc.)—all these contributed to the variety of his work without impairing either its artistic or its human integrity. "He narrates, and in this art he has no equal," says Gorky. Gorky who, incidentally, had learned a great deal from Leskov, also points out Leskov's profound love of Russia. Nor was it a small merit that Leskov preserved this love of Russia—together with his sense of humour and faith in life—even at the time of the general "Chekhovian" despondency in the 'eighties and early 'nineties.

Ignored or else deprecated by the critics while alive, Leskov yet succeeded in creating quite a large audience interested in his work. But he came really into his own at the beginning of this century, when he was taken up by a number of modernists. Alexey Remizov, a virtuoso of the word and of the *skaz* in Russian modernism, made Leskov (including his legendary and hagiographic motifs) the starting point for his own art. Another conspicuous follower of Leskov was Evgeny Zamyatin (he died in 1934) who excelled in the *skaz*-manner both before and after the revolution of 1917. Quite a few elements have been taken from Leskov by some of the best-known Soviet authors, especially during the early phase of Soviet fiction. The most popular living representative of the *skaz* is the Soviet author Michael Zoshchenko, whose shrewdly stylised sketches have been translated into all European languages. Told in the lower middle-class jargon and full of amusing pin-pricks, Zoshchenko's stories reflect the life of the Soviet citizens in its everyday humdrum: they are its unofficial history. The fact that, in spite of so many literary and other changes, the influence of Leskov's work still persists, is the best proof of its vitality. And there is no reason why its influence should not continue.

NINE

The Dramatic Art of Chekhov

I

CHEKHOV'S FAME SPREAD IN TWO WAVES—ONE THROUGH his stories, the other through his plays—and each of them brought something new with regard to subject-matter as well as the manner of presentation. Sincerity, simplicity and the sense of the obvious, bequeathed to Russian literature by Pushkin, reached in Chekhov's art that degree of truth and of elusive subtlety beyond which they could not possibly go. And since his impressionistic vision lent itself to pregnant brief statements rather than to carefully worked out disquisitions, Chekhov became a great master of the short story even before he was recognised as one of the pioneers of modern drama and the theatre.

As an interpreter of the "boring" 'eighties and early 'nineties, he depicted above all the weariness, the helpless despondency, of that period which he himself deplored as well as disliked. And if he, too, remained helpless and bewildered in the face of it all, he did so primarily because his artistic conscience would not allow him to accept, or even to preach, remedies in which he could not believe if he wanted to remain entirely honest with regard to himself and to his age. While comparing (in one of his letters to the founder and the editor of *Novoe Vremya*, A. Suvorin) himself and the authors of his time with those of the great realistic period, he said: "The best of them are realistic and paint life as it is; but because every line is permeated, as with a juice, by awareness of a purpose, you feel, besides life as it is, also life as it ought to be, and this captivates you. And we? We paint life as it is, and beyond that—no 'gee up' nor 'gee-down'. . . . Beyond that, even if you lashed us with whips, we could not go. We have neither immediate nor remote aims, and in our souls—a great emptiness. We have no politics, we do not believe in revolution, we have no God, we are not afraid of ghosts, and personally I have no fear even of death and blindness. He who desires nothing, hopes for nothing, and is afraid of nothing, cannot be an artist. Whether it is a disease or not the name does not matter; but it must be owned our situation is worse than bad. . . . I am at least clever enough not to hide my disease from myself, nor to cover up my emptiness with borrowed rags, such as the ideals of the 'sixties and so on. I shall not, like Garshin, throw myself down a flight of stairs, but neither am I going to delude myself with hopes of a better future. I am not to blame for my disease, nor am I called to cure myself, since this disease has, it must be supposed, some good purpose of its own hidden from us, and has not been sent in vain."*

The last line evidently leaves a loophole just wide enough to prevent him from falling into complete pessimism and to make him preserve a glimmer of hope which he kept secretly burning in spite of all. He had little in common with the sermonising Tolstoy or with the dissecting Dostoevsky, but felt a curious affinity with Turgenev the artist. It was above all Turgenev's lyrical impressionism and also his dispassionate aesthetic attitude towards life that left a mark upon Chekhov. Like Turgenev again, he may have been interested in the tasks and problems of the day, without however committing himself to any of them as an artist. He was explicit about this in another letter to Suvorin (October 1888) in which the passage in question runs as follows : "To deny that artistic creation involves problems and purposes would be to admit that an artist creates without premeditation, without design, under a spell. Therefore if an artist boasted to me of having written a story without a previously settled design, but by inspiration, I would call him a lunatic. You are right in demanding that an artist should take a conscious attitude to his work, but you confuse two conceptions: *the solution of a question and the correct setting of a question.* The latter alone is obligatory for an artist. It is for the judge to

* From *The Life and Letters of Anton Chekhov.* Translated and edited by S. S. Koteliansky and Philip Tomlinson (Cassell).

put the questions correctly; and the jurymen must decide, each one according to his taste."*

Keeping to this dictum, Chekhov abstained (with the exception of a short spell of Tolstoyanism, reflected in his longer story, *My Life*) from any "isms," any political and other parties, thereby preserving his artistic freedom to the end. "I am not a liberal, nor a conservative, nor a meliorist, nor a monk, nor an indifferentist," we read in a further letter of his (October 1889). "Pharisaism, stupidity and arbitrariness reign not in shopkeepers' houses and prisons alone. I detect them in science, in literature and in the younger generation. . . . For this reason I nurse no particular partiality for gendarmes, or butchers, or savants, or writers, or the younger generation. I look upon trademarks and labels as prejudices. My Holy of Holies is the human body, health, mind, talent, inspiration, love and the most absolute freedom—freedom from violence and falsehood in whatever they may be manifested. This is the programme I would follow if I were a great artist."*

II

HAVING SUCH PRONOUNCEMENTS OF HIS AT OUR DISPOSAL, we can perhaps more easily approach the spirit and the general character of Chekhov's work. The first thing likely to strike one is the dispassionate manner

* Op. cit.

in which he judged one of the drabbest periods of Russian life. Yet its very drabness was shown by him in a form both new and provocatively stimulating. This applies particularly to his plays the creation of which demanded a thorough overhaul of the traditional theatre and drama. Chekhov, incidentally, proclaimed (in one of his letters) the theatre of his time a "skin disease, a world of muddle, of stupidity and highfaluting" which should be swept away with a broom. He himself did not mind playing the part of such a broom in the 'eighties, when the only conspicuous reformer in this respect was Henrik Ibsen ; Gerhardt Hauptmann, Maurice Maeterlinck and others were yet to come. So Chekhov's pioneering was not devoid of courage even if he faltered, now and then, under the burden of his own innovations. Thus after the mixed reception of *Ivanov*, written in 1887 and first performed in 1889, he decided to abandon the theatre altogether. He made the same resolution after the unsuccessful production of *The Seagull* in October 1896. Fortunately, three years later his *Uncle Vanya* (a rewritten version of his previous and not very successful play, *The Wood Demon*) was staged by the Moscow Arts Theatre with unheard-of success. From now on Chekhov was closely associated with that theatre, so competently run by Stanislavsky. In 1901 he wrote for it *Three Sisters*, and in 1903—roughly a year before his death at the age of forty-four—*The Cherry Orchard*. In addition, he was responsible for the one-act play, *On the High Road* (anticipating as it were Gorky's famous *Lower Depths*), and for a few short but highly amusing vaudevilles and farces, such as *The Bear*, *The Proposal*, *The Jubilee*, etc. These can be regarded as dramatised counterparts of his humorous anecdotes and sketches, the boisterous laughter of which makes one think of the early stage of Gogol.

Chekhov's technique is of course widely different from that of Gogol. Yet, like Gogol, he too became haunted by the great Tedium as something inseparable from human existence. This attitude he expressed in accents entirely his own at an age when—partly because of the increased reaction after the murder of Alexander II, and partly because of the rapidly changing social-economic pattern—the whole of the Russian intelligentsia was plunged into a state of aimlessness and frustration. Feeling out of gear with the age, with the entire *Zeitgeist*, the best intellectuals of that period did not know what to do either with life or with themselves. And since Chekhov happened to be one of them, he was able to render their mood of bewilderment to perfection not only in his stories but also in his plays. His characters are "superfluous" in a more acute sense than those of Turgenev, for example. Their nostalgia, too, is different and comes frequently from their dissatisfaction with the very core of life. Their state of mind is further complicated by their feeling of isolation, by a strange inner barrier separating them even from those whom they once regarded as their nearest and dearest. Such above all is Ivanov, the principal character of the play under the same title. Treplev in *The Seagull*; Voinitsky, Astrov and Sonya in *Uncle Vanya* belong to the same category. So do Olga and Irina in *Three Sisters* ; and, to some extent, even the pathetically stupid owners of the bankrupt manor in *The Cherry Orchard.*

Chekhov connects, as a rule, this kind of helpless bewilderment not so much with weakness as with a surplus of sensitiveness, of thwarted refinement, on the part of the characters themselves. According to him, a highly sensitive person, confronted by the rough and ruthless competition in modern life, is almost doomed to failure, which, morally speaking, does him credit. On the other hand, success is a prerogative of the unscrupulous, the coarse and the vulgar. Chekhov, at any rate, looks upon it with a suspicion which only increases his sympathy and tenderness with regard to those *hommes manqués* who have been crushed because they expected or even demanded from life more than it could give. But the price they have to pay for their failure is, perhaps, not entirely in vain. Maybe they are paying the bill for the happiness of the generations to come, whose life will be less muddled and stupid than ours—a thought which does not alleviate the present trials, but confers upon them at least that possibility of a meaning which refuses to slam the door on all hope. Still, Chekhov's characters have to pay the bill. Quite a few of them know it and accept it in this spirit simply in order to avoid the temptation of utter nihilism.

"Those who will live a hundred or two hundred years after us, and who will despise us for having lived our lives so stupidly and tastelessly—they will, perhaps, find a means of being happy ; but we. . . . There is only one hope for you and me. The hope that when we are asleep in our graves we may, perhaps, be visited by pleasant visions."* Such is Dr. Astrov's comment in *Uncle Vanya*. But the same non-committal faith is voiced by Vershinin in *Three Sisters*; by Trofimov in *The Cherry Orchard*; and assumes a haunting aspect in the tragic symbolism of one of Chekhov's most powerful (and typical) narratives, *The Black Monk*. Chekhov himself must have looked for occasional solace in hopes of this kind, as one can judge from his letter to Serge Diaghilev (December, 1902), where he says: "Modern culture is but the beginning of a work for a great future, a work which will go on, perhaps, for ten thousand years, in order that mankind may, even in the remote future, come to know the truth of a real God—that is, not by guessing, not by seeking in Dostoevsky, but by perceiving clearly, as one perceives that twice two is four."

III

FLASHES OF SUCH FAITH DID NOT REDEEM, HOWEVER, the drabness of that present which Chekhov had to put up with and which he used, moreover, as the raw material for his stories and plays. The surprising thing is that he was able to transmute it into perfect art, the new devices of which are particularly worth studying in connection with his dramatic technique.

* All quotations from Chekhov's plays are taken from Mrs. Constance Garnett's translation of Chekhov's works (Chatto and Windus).

In the same way as Nekrasov once tried to de-poetise poetry, Chekhov did his best to de-theatralise the theatre by depriving it of everything "heroic," noisy, externally conspicuous and artificial. Yet in doing this he increased the effect of his plays in a strangely suggestive manner. In his first long play, *Ivanov*, he still depended to some extent on tradition, but he purposely abstained from a worked-out plot and made full use of what he called the "belletristic" as distinct from the dramatic method in the old sense. "Each act I finish as I do my stories," Chekhov says in a letter ; "I develop it quietly and calmly, but at the end I give a slap to the spectator. All my energy is centred on a few really strong passages, but the bridges connecting these passages are insignificant, weak and old-fashioned." The main hero is of course unheroic—a "superfluous" intellectual who, suddenly and through no fault of his own, has lost his hold upon life and feels, at the age of thirty-five, an old man.

"Exhausted, overstrained, broken, with my head heavy and my soul indolent, without faith, without love, without an object in life, I linger like a shadow among men and don't know what I am, what I am living for, what I want. . . . My brains do not obey me, nor my hands, nor my feet. My property is going to ruin, the forest is falling under the axe. My land looks at me like a deserted child. I expect nothing, I regret nothing ; my soul shudders with the fear of the morrow. . . . What is the matter with me ? To what depths am I making myself sink ? What has brought this weakness on me ?"

But there is no answer. Surrounded by fools, knaves and nonentities, he sinks deeper and deeper in his own aimlessness and cannot help offending even his devoted consumptive wife whom he used to adore. And when, after her death, he is free to marry Sasha, who had been in love with him all that time, he (again for no apparent reason) goes and shoots himself when on the point of taking her to the altar. We watch in him the tragedy of a sensitive man doomed to disintegrate, although he himself does not know why. There is no plot in the play, and even the normal logical causation seems to be absent ; yet as a picture of life turned into art—"on the wing" as it were—the piece is convincing and impressive.

In *The Seagull*, written some eight years later, Chekhov's peculiar technique is even more noticeable than in *Ivanov*. This time, too, the plot is replaced by a string of seemingly casual incidents, cemented by that lyrical "atmosphere" which both in his plays and his stories became the principal if not the only unifying factor. Here the tragedy of frustration in Treplev (a counterpart of Ivanov) and Nina is the more poignant because of all the trivialities leading up to it. While Nina, after her mistakes and disappointments, finds a shelter in the profession of an actress, Treplev cannot fill the void of his life even with his growing success in literature. These are his parting words to Nina after she had deserted him for a man who cared for her as little as he did for a shot seagull: "You have found your path, you know which way you are going, but I am still floating in a chaos of dreams and images, not knowing what use it is to anyone. I have no faith and I don't know what my vocation is." Chekhov again made use of the "belletristic" method but was not quite sure whether to approve of it or not, and he said so in a letter to Suvorin (November 1895): "I began it *forte* and finished it *pianissimo* against all rules of dramatic art. It came out like a story. I am more dissatisfied than satisfied with it, and, reading over my newborn piece, I become once more convinced that I am not a playwright at all." One can agree with him only in so far as he was not a playwright in the traditional sense, some further proofs of which he gave in his *Uncle Vanya*, *Three Sisters*, and *The Cherry Orchard.*

In *Uncle Vanya* we meet the same type of gentry-intellectuals, sinking in the morass of a trivial existence, as in *Ivanov* and *The Seagull*. Plot as such is replaced by a series of "scenes of country life in four acts." The "atmosphere" is all-important, while the subject is as simple as it can be. A retired professor, suffering from conceit and gout, comes with his beautiful second wife Elena to settle down on the estate, where his brother-in-law, Voinitsky (Uncle Vanya), and his daughter from the first marriage, Sonya, have been toiling for years in order to increase his income. Thinking the world of the professor's fame and learning, Voinitsky has spent the whole of his adult life in serving him—only to discover in the end that the supposedly great man is nothing but an ignorant, puffed-up nonentity. Voinitsky, a weary middle-aged failure, realises his mistake, but the lost years can no longer be retrieved. To make things worse, he is in love with Elena, who is emotionally too indolent to respond to his advances, or even to those of the younger and more interesting Astrov—still in the process of going to seed. As though lost in his own void, he is frightened of the present and the future. "I am forty-seven. If I live to be sixty, I have another thirteen years. It's a long time. How am I to get through those thirteen years? What shall I do? How am I to fill them up? . . ." In his rancour Voinitsky fires two shots at the pitiably frightened celebrity and, having missed, thinks of suicide. But it all ends peacefully. The learned professor and his wife depart. Life returns to its old routine. Both Voinitsky and Sonya (whose secret love for Astrov is frustrated for good) find an escape—of which they are fully conscious this time—in their petty drudgery about the estate.

Three Sisters is written in a similar vein, with an even increased amount of lyrical overtones. Again there is no plot. We are introduced to three sisters—members of the intelligentsia (in this case the cultured higher officers' class in the 'eighties), who, after their father's death, have remained stuck in a provincial town they loathe. Their determination to return to Moscow, where they were born, only expresses their desire for a full and throbbing life. But the provincial morass is stronger. Neither they nor their brother, who is preparing for a learned career, succeed in extricating themselves. Instead of living, they are compelled only to exist. "I am nearly twenty-four," complains Irina. "I have been working for years, my brains are drying up, I am getting thin and old and ugly and there is nothing, nothing, not the slightest satisfaction, and time is passing, and one feels that one is moving away and being drawn into the depths. I am in despair and I don't know how it is I am alive and have not killed myself yet." It is no fault of theirs that all their efforts are futile and that things go from bad to worse. Their brother, moreover, marries a mean and vulgar *petite bourgeoise* who openly deceives him with another man. And as in *Uncle Vanya*, Chekhov ends the play again *pianissimo*, with the apparent acceptance of the all-round frustrations and blind-alley, camouflaged by hard work.

The tone is somewhat brighter in *The Cherry Orchard* —that dramatised string of comic and semi-tragic incidents. The bankruptcy of the irresponsibly carefree, or rather careless, Ranevskaya and her brother Gayev is here symbolic of the inner as well as external bankruptcy of that gentry-class which not so long ago had dominated the whole of Russian life. Ranevskaya's country-house, together with its magnificent cherry orchard, is sold to the self-made businessman Lopakhin —the son of a former serf; and the first thing the new owner does is to fell the orchard in order to make room for a housing-estate planned out on a most profitable basis. Lopakhin thus emerges as a new social force— a capitalist on a large scale. But the "eternal student" and revolutionary Trofimov has little respect for and less fear of him. "I can get on without you. I can pass by you." He is still young enough to flatter himself with the illusion that he, and not the "practical" money-grabbing Lopakhin, is in the front ranks of humanity even if Lopakhin is the only one who triumphs at the end of the play.

The Cherry Orchard was written specially for Stanislavsky who regarded it as Chekhov's best dramatic work. Its first performance took place in January, 1904. But its technique was too new and too subtle to captivate the public at once, even the public of the Moscow Arts Theatre.

IV

TO SUM UP THAT TECHNIQUE IN A FEW SENTENCES IS not an easy matter. On the whole, Chekhov stands outside that tradition of Russian dramatic art which goes from Fonvizin (eighteenth century)—via Kapnist and Griboyedov—to Gogol's *Government Inspector*, even if Chekhov's farcical one-acters are still reminiscent of Gogol. On the other hand, his "belletristic," or perhaps static, method had quite an interesting Russian precedent in Turgenev's *A Month in the Country* which, like *Uncle Vanya*, could be called "scenes from country life" rather than a play in the traditional style. Also Alexander Ostrovsky—the greatest Russian playwright during the realistic period—may have contributed certain elements to the Chekhovian drama, however different Ostrovsky's aims may have been from those of Chekhov.* As an innovator Chekhov had more in common with Ibsen (whom he admired) than with any Russian, but again with reservations.

Like Ibsen in his later plays, he too discarded the old-fashioned plot and reduced the external action to a minimum. Yet he replaced the latter not so much by the psychological inner tension à la Ibsen as by an accumulation of that lyrical-impressionistic "atmosphere" which keeps the seemingly disjointed incidents together. The curious similarity between the symbolic use of the seagull in Chekhov's play and that of the wild duck in the well-known drama by Ibsen may, of course, not be purely accidental. Analogies could also be found elsewhere—for instance, between the ending of *Three Sisters* (with the departing soldiers and music in the distance) and that of Ibsen's *The Lady of the Sea*, not to mention Chekhov's frequent use of the double dialogue, the spoken words of which serve as a mask for what one actually wants to say. On the other hand, there are quite a few differences between these two pioneers of modern drama. For one thing, in his disregard of the conventional plot Ibsen relegated the tragic guilt of his hero to the past (i.e. to the time before the play began) and, therefore, concentrated only on the psychological *dénouement* as seen through the workings of the hero's conscience, tossed as a rule between two contradictory sets of moral values. The climax is expressed through the

* Ostrovsky's theatre is above all of manners of the old-fashioned merchant-class in Moscow and also in the provinces. The local colour and the ethnographic element played a most conspicuous part in his works.

hero's inner change due to his sudden perception of a truth which gives a new direction to his will, to his entire personality, even if he may not be strong enough to live up to it, as we see in *Rosmersholm*, *The Master-builder*, *John Gabriel Borkman*, and *When we Dead Awaken*. In Ibsen's psychological plays the principal character invariably remains in the limelight, while the structure itself is determined by the moral catharsis occurring in his consciousness.

Chekhov proceeds differently. Having discarded the old plot, he does not replace it by a conflict of inner values in the manner of Ibsen for the simple reason that his very point of departure is the bankruptcy of all values. Nor do we find in him that logical and psychological unity in which Ibsen the playwright excelled to the end. On the contrary, Chekhov depicted the casualness of a disintegrating life in that seemingly casual way which Tolstoy once referred to (rather disapprovingly) as a "scattered composition." Yet there was a system in Chekhov's method, as well as an inner unity underneath the externally "scattered" bits and slices of life. It was precisely in the skill with which he achieved this unity that Chekhov proved to be one of the inimitable masters in the whole of European modernism.

V

IN HIS ENDEAVOUR TO SHOW THE TRAGIC NATURE OF ordinary everyday existence by means of the "atmosphere" as the main cementing factor, Chekhov went a long way to abolish the old method of acting. In this respect his plays are, perhaps, even more difficult to handle than those of Ibsen ; but the Moscow Arts Theatre (the beginnings of which are so closely bound up with Chekhov) did full justice to them on the stage : by realising how much their success depended on nuances and all sorts of psychological imponderables, not to mention the importance of the pauses, of the tempo, as well as of the deeper "symbolic" side of gestures and intonation. After all, it was not for nothing that the impressionist Chekhov was proclaimed by Andrey Bely a precursor of Russian symbolism.

Yet Chekhov's symbolism is more vague and elusive than, say, that of Ibsen. And, perhaps, more organic, too. As it springs not from any calculated literary devices, but from the author's total attitude towards life, it often becomes one of the primary ingredients of the "atmosphere" permeating his works. This "atmosphere" may be tragic enough in itself, but the characters acting and moving in it are either too fatalistic or else too pathetic to be really tragic. In contrast to Ibsen's characters, they have neither enough faith nor enough stamina even to dare to fight for—let alone shape, their own destinies.

This need not be, however, a drawback. Exceptional material lends itself more easily to artistic processes than the apparently uninteresting and drab everyday actuality. The uniqueness of Chekhov is due to the skill with which he proved that the very drabness of life can be turned into great and significant art. But he was able to do this only because of his wellnigh clairvoyant perception of the complexities lurking under the most ordinary crust of life. His principal strength was in his understanding of human weakness. And he showed us that weakness in a subtle, dispassionate light, which was itself one of the major contributions to the sensibility of our time.

TEN

Maxim Gorky

I

THE SPAN OF TIME DIVIDING US FROM MAXIM GORKY'S death is now big enough to allow us to see his life-work in its proper perspective from a literary as well as social point of view. In his case it would be difficult to separate one from the other, since the pathos permeating his writings was not so much of an aesthetic as of a social and reformatory order, but with a difference. The artist and the reformer were neither antagonistic in him as they were in Tolstoy ; nor were they mixed up as was so often the case with H. G. Wells. In Gorky the two propensities converged and, instead of disturbing, seemed to strengthen one another. His very choice of themes was conditioned by his protest against the kind of life he saw around, and he depicted the ugly side of reality in a spirit widely different from that of Gogol and his followers. Instead of feeding on a rancorous negation of life, he permeated his writings with his strongest urge—the urge to turn the whole of existence into something of which human beings need no longer feel ashamed. Gorky's literary work can, therefore, best be understood in conjunction with the role he played in the social and political life of Russia during the most fateful transition years in her history. The uniqueness of his role was enhanced by the fact that he was the first major Russian author who had risen from the "lower depths" of the social ladder and had started life as a proletarian, indeed as an outcast. Apart from a few months in a shabby elementary school at Nizhny Novgorod, he knew only one other school—that of life. But he made such good use of it that, at the age of thirty, he was already one of the most popular authors in his native country, and before long his name became a household word—more, a slogan all the world over.

This alone puts Gorky among the arresting figures of our time. Yet if we want to gauge the full value of his work and personality, we must approach him in the light of the conditions prevailing in Russia at the beginning of the 'nineties of the last century, when he (at that time a railway worker of twenty-four) had his first story printed. The Tsarist Russia of that period was one of the most class-ridden countries in Europe—a state of things which was further aggravated by her rapidly growing industry. The abolition of serfdom in 1861 had made the peasants independent of their former landlords, but as it had not given them enough land to subsist on with their growing families, the landless surplus of the village population began to flood the town-factories, often under the most appalling conditions. The position of the factory workers was rendered more precarious by the lack of proper organisations among the working masses themselves whose cultural level was still too low for any initiative of this kind. True enough, in Russia there had existed, in the second half of the last century, a peculiar brand of "populist" or agrarian socialism, but it was confined mainly to the intelligentsia. It represented a belated (if somewhat sentimental) effort on the part of the "repentant" intellectuals from among the gentry to atone for the injustice under which the serfs had smarted for generations. This "populism" pinned its faith in a better future exclusively to the peasants rooted in the soil, and not to the town-proletarians. It was, moreover, based on the false premise that Russia, in contrast to Europe, could by-pass the capitalist phase and jump, so to speak, from her primitive conditions straight into an agrarian socialist millennium.

Meanwhile, the industrial proletariat in the bigger Russian towns was on the increase. From the 'seventies onwards it even began to organise itself—first on a professional and later also on a political and ideological basis. The consolidation of this process coincided with the blossoming out of Gorky's talent. He even became, at the beginning of this century, one of the principal literary and moral forces behind all the activities connected with the working class movement in Russia—activities which reached their first climax in the abortive rising of 1905 and their triumph in the revolution of 1917. It is the background of these two revolutions, with all the toil which preceded, conditioned and followed them, that can provide us with a reliable approach to such a phenomenon as Maxim Gorky.

II

BORN IN 1868 INTO AN ARTISAN FAMILY AT NIZHNY Novgorod, now named after him, Alexey Maximovich Peshkov (Gorky's real name) soon became an orphan and stayed until the age of ten with his grandparents. His grandfather, who had a dye workshop, went bankrupt and the boy was sent to a footwear store, from which he duly escaped. For a while he served as a dish-washer on a Volga steamer, but this was only the beginning of an endless series of other professions: from a sweated worker in a baker's shop to a street pedlar; from a fisherman on the Caspian Sea to a railway worker at some remote god-forsaken stations; from a petty clerk in a lawyer's office to a debutant in literature; and from a provincial journalist to a world-famous author. In the course of all those changes and peregrinations it was in Kazan alone (where he mixed with the radical-minded undergraduates) that Gorky found a congenial atmosphere, but not for long. He had to earn his living, and there were times when he was a regular down-and-out. In 1887 he made an attempt at suicide, but his life was saved in the nick of time by the skill of a hospital surgeon. His frequent companions in those days were the social outcasts; yet far from despising them he tried to understand their fate and to fathom through it his own attitude towards life. Years later he confessed to having felt among them "like a piece of iron in glowing coal—every day filled me with a mass of sharp, burning impressions. I saw before me people nakedly greedy, people with rough instincts—and I liked their bitterness about life, I liked their ironically hostile attitude towards everything in the world, and also their carefree attitude towards themselves." There was a great deal of moral and social callousness among them, but Gorky's actively idealistic and reformatory temperament—perhaps the most typical feature of his character—was his surest guide through the vicissitudes of life. He also realised that before taking any part in the fight against the ugliness and cruelty of existence he had much to learn. So he missed no opportunity of making up for the deficiencies of his education. Yet even after his first story, *Makar Chudra*, had appeared in a Caucasian newspaper at Tiflis, Gorky was not quite sure whether writing was his actual vocation. He continued his literary apprenticeship for another few years, working for the most part on the Volga papers, and his talent kept maturing at such a pace that in 1898 he was able to publish the first two volumes of his collected stories. Their success was immediate. Many people were shocked by the novelty of Gorky's themes, by his tone and manner, but they all read him. And they realised there and then that a new literary force had arisen which could be either accepted or rejected, but which could by no means be ignored.

The significance of this force was the greater because the decade preceding Gorky's debut was one of Chekhovian tiredness and disappointment. The resigned melancholy, so typical of Chekhov's stories and plays, is reflected in a number of his older contemporaries: in the writer Garshin (who committed suicide) ; in the nostalgic poetry of Nadson and Apukhtin ; in the paintings of Levitan ; in the music of Tchaikovsky. The only thriving proposition in those days was "business" which, from the 'eighties onwards, made rapid strides (especially under the leadership of such a financial wizard as Count Witte) and turned quite a large portion of the gentry into its votaries. A number of intellectuals hoped to find an escape in Tolstoy's moral perfectionism. Others looked for it in a beefy philistine indifference to everything except comfort and money. Others again shut themselves in the "ivory towers" of that decadent art which celebrated its first triumphs in Russia in the middle of the same decade that witnessed the challenge of Maxim Gorky. The whole of Gorky's work can in fact be described as one long challenge. But it was also a tonic potent enough to stir up a new will and a new hope even among those who had never dared to will or to hope.

III

GORKY'S FIRST AND SECOND PERIODS, ROUGHLY FROM 1892 until 1901, bore the stamp of romantic defiance to all those forces which tend to cripple life and to dehumanise the vast majority of human beings. For this reason he chose a somewhat loud and often rather flowery style, charged with the fury of a "stormy petrel," as he was named at the outset. He also introduced into his stories such characters as were likely to express his own defiance and protest. We find among them gipsies, Tatar shepherds, vagabonds, smugglers, thieves, fishermen, ragged proletarians and people from the "lower depths" in general—people who have never had the slightest reason for being in love with the existing order of things. Resentful, provocative in word and in action, most of them keep to the philosophy of safety last. At the same time they have ideas of human worth which are entirely their own and do not necessarily tally with those of their social superiors, about whom they have no illusions. The consciousness of class-division and class antagonism thus reached in Gorky's characters an acuteness which was itself something new in Russian fiction, and this remained one of his permanent features. Some of Gorky's critics were inclined to see in him, during that period, a kind of Nietzsche from the gutter. But this was a superficial notion. Gorky, who had passed through the gutter and had risen so high above it, was anxious to abolish the gutter of life altogether. In this consisted his strength and his weakness : strength because such an aim increased his creative *verve* ; and weakness, because it imparted to him a didactic and, at times, schematic "purpose." Anyway, he worked in two directions. One of these was the way of protest in the name and on behalf of the victims, while the other took the form of a series of pictures of the gutter itself and of the "creatures that once were human beings"—to use his pregnant but untranslatable Russian phrase *byvshie lyudi.*

Most of his early material was taken by Gorky from his own experiences and observations. And like Leskov before him, he keenly appreciated the incident as such, which he imbued with a provocatively romantic and also provocatively didactic strain. This applies even to his pictures of the "lower depths," where his realism of indictment had full sway. For no matter how degraded the people described, he lost no opportunity of stressing the potential excellence of the human material thus crushed by the social system. One of his expedients of intensified characterisation was the kind of contrast one finds in his early story called *Chelkash.* Its hero, a carefree thief and outcast, has no respect for anybody or anything, yet at bottom he is a broad, generous type—a potential aristocrat by nature. His helper in a somewhat risky adventure is a pious little peasant who in the end turns out to be a worm—quite capable of murdering his companion in order to gratify his own greed for money. As a result the outcast Chelkash turns out to be much better human material than the acquisitive God-fearing peasant who can think in no other terms except those of property.

Nowhere, however, is Gorky's faith in the latent value of the social outcast stressed to better purpose than in his story, *Twenty-six Men and a Girl*, written in

1899. Twenty-six "creatures that once were men" toil like slaves in a filthy suburban bakery, mercilessly exploited by their boss and despised even by those workers whose pay and social status are slightly higher than theirs. The only ray of light in that squalor is a pretty innocent girl who passes every morning by their den in order to collect some pretzel buns. All the twenty-six slaves fall in love with her—ideally and chivalrously, since she embodies that element of decency and beauty of life which still secretly smoulders at the bottom of their hearts. But even this last illusion is soiled when, one day, they find out that she has succumbed to the charms of a swaggering vulgarian, and their brutal revenge only proves the depth of their disappointment.

It was not for nothing that the author of such narratives assumed the nickname Maxim the Bitter (Gorky means "bitter," or rather "embittered," in Russian). But since his bitterness only increased his fight against the filth and cruelty of life, he could not help being didactic even to the extent of turning many of his characters into mouthpieces of his own ideas. Hence his frequent preachings, his love for sententious formulae, his exuberance and—in contrast to Chekhov—his use of full colours.

It may have been for this reason that, in a letter, Chekhov referred to Gorky as a deep and thinking author but carrying "much unnecessary ballast—for example his provincialism." In another letter, addressed to Gorky himself (in December 1898) Chekhov expressed his friendly and at the same time severe criticism of Gorky's style in these terms: "In my opinion you do not use sufficient restraint. You are like a spectator in the theatre who expresses his rapture so unreservedly that he prevents both himself and others from listening. Particularly is this lack of restraint felt in the descriptions of Nature with which you interrupt your dialogues; when one reads those descriptions one wishes they were more compact, shorter, put, say, into two or three lines. The frequent mention of tenderness, whispering, velvetiness, and so on, gives to these descriptions a certain character of rhetoric and monotony—and they chill the reader, almost tire him. Lack of restraint is felt also in the description of women and in the love scenes. It is not vigour, nor breadth of touch, but plain lack of reserve."*

This is a fair criticism, especially of Gorky at his worst. But one should not forget that Gorky was a self-made author of a new type who wrote deliberately for a new type of reader, emerging among the working classes themselves. This self-made reader (if one is allowed to call him so) needed a different approach as well as different food from that offered by the intelligentsia literature of the period. He found both in Gorky's writings.

IV

GORKY PROVED A GREATER STIMULUS IN THIS RESPECT than any other Russian author. And when he was

* *The Life and Letters of Anton Chekhov* (Cassell).

at the height of success, he not only did not dissociate himself from the working masses but, on the contrary, took a lead in their movement, knowing that his voice was likely to be heard far and wide. This necessitated, however, an enlargement of his themes, which now included a deeper criticism of society and of the class-struggle, beginning with his first longer work, *Foma Gordeyev* (1899). The background of this novel is the close-fisted but already decaying commercial bourgeoisie in a Volga town. Realising the emptiness of such existence with its opulent animality, the principal character Foma, a member of the same class, feels out of tune with it. One can see in him a not very successful transposition of the "superfluous man" from the gentry to a different social layer. For Gorky's Foma is the only anaemic character in the novel. He is certainly much less alive and impressive than his enterprising father. But to make up for him, the author brings in some of those dissatisfied characters whose moods and activities are dictated by a clearer awareness of what they want and why. Critical realism inspired by a romantic faith and aiming at a complete renewal of life, now became Gorky's favourite genre. This was partly the reason why he tried his strength in dramatic activities as well. Aware of the influence that could be exercised from the stage, he wrote in 1901 his first play, *The Petit-Bourgeois* (*Meshchane*). Here he challenged the philistinism of the more prosperous artisan-class itself, the only redeeming feature of which he found in the younger generation consciously working for a new life and a new era to come. About a year later, Gorky's second play *The Lower Depths* (*Na dne*) became a world success, partly because of its subject-matter. The author introduces us here to the inmates of a dosshouse, yet amidst all the misery and degradation of those "ex-humans" one can still perceive sparks of humanity, strangely mixed with their dreams of a different life. The indignation permeating the play is social as well as ethical, and his brutal frankness about the depth of human misery can have an overwhelming effect, if well acted.

Gorky was by then a member of the Russian social-democratic party which he joined in 1902. He became something of a focus for the revolutionary activities before and during the eventful year of 1905, which did not prevent him, however, from finishing two more plays, *The Holiday Makers* and *Children of the Sun*. Both were rather topical at the moment: they treated the old problem of the intelligentsia and the people from a new angle. Gorky's attitude towards the intellectuals of his own period was, on the whole, negative. He thought the bulk of them effete and the more "superfluous" because they were already despised by the people themselves who could not help seeing the emptiness of their existence. In another piece, *The Barbarians*, the two intellectuals—this time two engineers, building a railway through a remote provincial town—succeed in corrupting the whole town as if it had been invaded by a barbarian horde. The only hope Gorky could see was the new intellectual arising from the masses and courageously working for a better future. This, at any rate, is the leading idea of *The Holiday Makers*, which—let it be said in fairness—is far from being a good play. The problem of the intelligentsia is tackled somewhat differently in *Children of the Sun*. Here we see the elite of the mind; but since this elite is severed from the masses, the danger of it being ousted from life altogether is there and, as Gorky shows, abounds in dreadful possibilities. Finally, in *The Enemies* (1906) he considered the proletariat, in its struggle against capitalism, the principal and perhaps the only guarantee of a better future. Gorky's plays were being successfully staged all over Russia at a time when Chekhov's dramatic art had at last found its proper interpretation in the Moscow Arts Theatre. Even more interesting is the fact that Gorky, whose explosive manner was so different from that of Chekhov, actually adopted Chekhov's technique of a "static" drama. It was a risky step on the part of such a dynamic personality as Gorky. More than once he was in danger of turning Chekhov's delicate lyrical pastel into a didactic oleograph. At his best, however, he managed to get away with it in spite of that—in his *Lower Depths*, for instance.

V

GORKY'S DRAMATIC WORKS MARKED A FURTHER STAGE in his endeavour to make literature itself active in clearing away the ballast of the old life. He also became the promoter of the publishing firm *Znanie* (Knowledge) as a gathering point for all those authors who were anxious to preserve the good traditions of Russian realism and yet make their own writings socially significant—in plain defiance of the detached "highbrow" aestheticism just then in the ascendant. The success of this venture surpassed all expectations. A number of talented young authors — Kuprin, Andreyev, Bunin—wrote for *Znanie*, the association with which soon became an entrance ticket to fame.

Gorky's influence had grown by then enough to make the authorities perturbed. Having already been in prison on many occasions, Gorky regarded further experiences of this kind as a matter of course. After the blood-bath of January 9th, 1905, when a peaceful procession of workers wishing to lay their grievances before the Tsar had been massacred by the troops almost within the precincts of the Winter Palace, Gorky was arrested once again. But his fame was by this time so great that violent protests followed from all over Europe, under the pressure of which he had to be released. But he remained as incorrigible as ever. In October 1905 he founded the socialist paper *New Life* which, edited by Lenin himself, existed for some five weeks before it was clamped down by the police. It was in this paper that Gorky's series of attacks on the modern bourgeois mentality appeared. He also played one of the leading parts in the Moscow rising. And when the revolution of 1905 had proved a failure, Gorky gave all his support to those who had decided to continue their fight underground. He travelled in both Europe and America in order to increase the funds of his party. Then he settled down on the island of Capri where he worked for a resumption of the struggle and wrote his revolutionary novel *The Mother* (1907-08)—his first big work since 1905.

An important social document and a propaganda novel rather than a work of art, *The Mother* depicts the Russian workers' struggle for their rights at the beginning of this century. The events described actually took place in 1902 in the factory district of Sormov near Nizhny Novgorod, and the two leading characters of the novel—the young worker Vlasov and his widowed mother—were among Gorky's personal friends. The early chapters, which are the best, show the low level of the old-time factory workers: their sloth, apathy, drunken rows and hooliganism. Then, gradually, a new set of social values and ideals, with which some of them come into contact, produces an almost miraculous change. The change does not remain mere theory, but is soon translated into an active determination to work for a better future. Gorky makes us follow the various phases of this process. We see how revolutionary organisations are formed from within. Further, we witness the clashes between the workers and the employers; the onslaught of the reactionary powers-that-be. But the struggle goes on, and the tenacity on the part of the workers grows in proportion to their setbacks. The chief impression conveyed by this novel is the incredible vitality of Russian workers once they have embraced a cause in which they believe. Yet it is here in particular that Gorky's didactic propensity asserts itself to the uttermost—propaganda is mixed with, rather than sublimated by, art—which did not prevent the novel from having a tremendous effect upon the working-class consciousness in Russia as well as abroad, notably in France and Germany, at a time when even the liberal bourgeoisie of those two countries had turned against Gorky.

VI

LESS THAN A YEAR AFTER *The Mother*, GORKY published one of his strangest and in its own way most fascinating books, called simply *A Confession*. Written in the first person, it reveals a typical Russian roamer: not the anarchic vagabond of Gorky's earlier stories, but an almost Leskovian hero—deeply rooted in his country and united through a kind of *participation mystique* with the eternally toiling, eternally yearning and seeking, "God-seeking" folk masses. Its pages vibrate with that innate love for the land and the people which is a matter of one's deepest instincts rather than any ideologies, and which was so typical of Leskov. Also the beauty of the spacious Russian landscape is conjured up with all its charm. It is Gorky's most poetic book about Russia—probably inspired by nostalgia for his native country. The distance which lay between him and Russia made him, however, see and judge also the negative side of

Russian life in its proper perspective. This in its turn was responsible for the increase in Gorky's realism of indictment, as we find it in his narratives, *The Town of Okurov* and *The Life of Matvey Kozhemyakin* (1909-11).

These two works are interdependent. *The Town of Okurov* is called (like Leskov's *Cathedral Folk*) a chronicle. It deals with the same remote provincial Russia as Leskov's famous work, but as it shows only its reverse side, it is more in the line of Saltykov-Shchedrin's scathing invectives. The hero of the narrative is the town itself. There may be a difference between its "respectable" part and its destitute suburb, yet in both, life is equally drab, senseless and squalid. The only diversion that now and then interrupts its monotony is crime, or the kind of shabby drama which forms the climax of the narrative at the moment when the echoes of the revolution of 1905 are beginning to stir up even this god-forsaken hole. A typical chronicle is also *The Life of Matvey Kozhemyakin.* Gorky takes here a lower-middle-class inhabitant of the same Okurov and unrolls before us his existence during some fifty years of continuous frustrations. Sapped from the outset, Kozhemyakin is essentially a decent fellow, all the time groping for something worth living for, though without guidance or any tangible results. He feels as "superfluous" in his surroundings as Foma Gordeyev felt in his, and is equally unable to cope with their crushing effect. His death, which is only the last act of a long and slow process of dying, takes place when the revolutionary outburst of 1905 seems to promise a different era. To quote an entry from Kozhemyakin's own diary shortly before he died: "New workers have now appeared in our life —with hearts full of love for this earth which we have besmirched; they are living ploughs which will furrow God's field deeply, down to its very heart and will make it glow and blossom up with a new sun, warm and kindly to all men, bringing to them a happy life."

After some three hundred pages of "Chekhovian" futility, but depicted with Gorky's ruggedness and indignation, the final note of this work is one of faith and hope. And such an attitude was typical of Gorky even during the stifling era of "Stolypin's collar,"* as the noose of the hangman's rope was ironically called at the time. There was, of course, Tolstoy's protest—in his pamphlet *I Cannot be Silent*; there was also a virulent indictment by Korolenko, but nothing could stay the triumph of reaction, which gradually became undermined by its own excesses. Of all the major authors Gorky alone refused to give in. His criticism of the Okurov Russia became increasingly violent, and so did his insistence on a radical change. Even his most significant literary achievements between the two revolutions, *Childhood* and *In the World*—the first two parts of his autobiographical trilogy—are an indictment of those conditions which can cripple one's tender years as had been the case with Gorky himself. The only bright spot in the nightmare of his early life was his granny, whose portraiture in the book is unforgettable.

* The prime-minister Stolypin was regarded as being chiefly responsible for the epidemic of executions after the triumph of the reaction in 1905.

Thanks to the amnesty on the occasion of the tercentenary of the Romanovs in 1913, Gorky was allowed to return to Russia where he stayed all through the first World War. But as he was far from enthusiastic either about the war or its behind-the-scenes, his subversive activities continued. In the winter of 1915 he started a big monthly, *The Annals* (*Letopis*), the spirit of which was anti-bourgeois, anti-war, and anti-imperialistic. Then the revolution of 1917 came which, with all its defects and horrors, put as it were overnight before the whole of the world the cardinal problem of our age, namely: Is mankind going to serve the capitalist system and be dehumanised by it, or can we make capital itself serve the purposes of humanity? Russia was the first big country to give a definite answer to this dilemma, and her answer coincided, more or less, with the one Gorky had all the time been fighting for. His two bugbears, the decayed capitalist bourgeoisie and the decayed section of the intelligentsia, were swept away by the tidal wave of the revolution which, for the first time, opened up the untapped energies of the masses inhabiting one sixth of our globe. To quote Gorky's own words, "Now the entire Russian people is taking part in history—this is an event of cardinal importance, and it is from this angle that we ought to judge all the bad and good things, all our joys and sorrows."

This does not mean that Gorky approved of everything that was taking place in those fateful days. In his resuscitated periodical, *New Life*, he indulged in a series of polemics with the Bolsheviks and with

Lenin himself Appalled by the excesses let loose by the revolution, he insisted more than ever on raising the cultural level of the masses and, after his teconciliation with Lenin in 1918, he did his utmost ro achieve this desired end. He was one of the principal organisers of help to all writers and savants, regardless of their political allegiance, and this was not a small matter during the general shortage and famine. Gorky also stepped in as a defender of cultural continuity at a time when a number of people were advocating a purely proletarian culture. It was he in particular who turned against such narrow-minded sectarianism and demanded that the best elements bequeathed by the former intelligentsia-culture should be assimilated by the Soviet masses and creatively blended with what they themselves can give to the world. Further, even before the duress of the Civil War was over, he set up a far-reaching undertaking, the aim of which was to present the Soviet people with the classical works of world-literature, translated and commentated by experts. In this manner he became a bridge not only between the Soviets and the former Russian culture, but also between the Soviets and the culture of the world.

Whether Gorky welcomed or not all the single aspects connected with the birth-pangs of the New Russia does not really matter. What matters is that he fully realised the impact of the new *direction* given to world-history by the Revolution of 1917. After all, Tsarist Russia had been a diseased organism in need of a surgical operation, and the operations performed by history are usually done without anaesthetics. So we must not be surprised that, in spite of repeated squabbles and misunderstandings, Gorky threw in his lot with the Bolshevist system—a step which, several years after, he explained in a private letter as follows: "Do I side with the Bolsheviks who deny freedom? Yes, I do, because I stand for the freedom of all people who work honestly, but I am against the freedom of parasites and harmful babblers. I used to argue with the Bolsheviks and to oppose them in 1917, when it seemed to me that they were unlikely to win over the peasants driven by the war into anarchy, and that a conflict with them threatened to ruin the workers' party itself. Then I came to the conclusion that I was wrong, and now I am fully convinced that the Russian people, however much it be hated by the governments of Europe and whatever its economic difficulties as a result of that hatred, has entered the phase of its regeneration."

VII

ALL THESE ACTIVITIES ON THE PART OF GORKY WERE so much hampered by his bad health (chronic tuberculosis) that in the winter of 1921 he undertook a cure abroad, first in Germany and later in Southern Italy, whence he returned to Russia in 1928. During that time his literary output remained as abundant as ever and included some of his maturest works: *My Uni-*

versities, his novels *The Artamonov Business* and *The Life of Klim Samgin*, as well as his play *Yegor Bulichov*.

My Universities refers to Gorky's hard school of life during his years of adolescence and early manhood. It completes his autobiographical trilogy and (like the first two parts) is crammed with incidents, portraits and descriptions, done without any self-pity and on a high literary level. Like the previous two volumes, it is invaluable for an understanding of Gorky's development and of his personality in general. As for *The Artamonov Business* (1925), the very title of this artistically most perfect novel he ever wrote suggests that, once again, we are taken back to the moneyed bourgeoisie of the old regime. Like *The Forsyte Saga*, it is the history of a big firm spread over three successive generations. Stained by a crime at its beginning, the factory founded by the enterprising ex-serf Artamonov soon expands into a prosperous concern. But the disintegrating process has already set in with the second generation, while in the third the Artamonov dynasty is deposed by the Revolution of 1917. The firm becomes national property, and a new era begins—at least for the workers. A similar motif must have been in Gorky's mind when he planned his unfinished dramatic trilogy of which *Yegor Bulichov* was to be the first part. Here, too, as in *The Artamonov Business*, we see the new era knocking at the door of a prosperous but corrupt firm, only this time the starting point is the chaos prevailing during the First World War and the February Revolution. The cunningly unscrupulous Yegor Bulichov is something of a symbol of the old system and, like the system itself, suffers from a mortal illness. When at last the song of the rising masses bursts from the street into the room of the dying invalid, he knows that his time is up. "What is it? The burial service singing me out of the world!" And so it is. The burial service for the entire historical period which he represents.

There still remains *The Life of Klim Samgin*—the biggest and most ambitious of Gorky's works. It is in four parts, the last of which remained unfinished. At a first glance it may look like a more detailed intelligentsia counterpart of his petit-bourgeois chronicle, *Matvey Kozhemyakin.* But it turns out to be something much bigger: a chronicle of Russian life during some forty years—roughly from 1880 until 1917. Gorky attempted to give here a cross-section of practically all the Russian classes as seen by a typical offspring of the intelligentsia, Klim Samgin. Klim himself serves as the centre for an amazing variety of characters, many of them in the course of their development, or else depicted in their reactions to all the phases and crises of Russian history during those years. Particularly good is the first part, showing the early development of a whole generation in a big provincial centre. The second and third parts, dealing with the Russo-Japanese War and the events of 1905, may at times be drawn out (by lengthy discussions), but they are of paramount documentary value. The same can be said of the unfinished fourth part, which brings events up to the February

Revolution of 1917. Such a long and ambitious chronicle of Russian life is bound to be uneven, but its finest portions show Gorky at his best. The work is a masterpiece of critical realism. Yet however realistic Gorky's method, one feels underneath it —here perhaps more than in any of his former writings —an active idealist aiming at a transformation of the existing pattern of life. Apart from his descriptive passages, Gorky excels here also as a portrait painter and psychologist. In no other work did he give such a number of complicated, even "Dostoevskian" characters as here, beginning with the principal hero Klim Samgin, whose life is an abbreviated and somewhat symbolic image of that liberal intelligentsia which was thrown out of its unfulfilled historical mission by the Revolution of 1917. It was through him that Gorky tried to analyse not only the external but the inner reasons why during the most crucial period of Russian history the intelligentsia proved unable to lead the country and the nation through the crisis. This is why it was necessary to show—in retrospect— the entire development of the generation represented by Klim. We see him first as a child growing up in a family with the "populist" traditions. After his Grammar School years in a provincial town, we follow him as a student to Petersburg, to Moscow, then as a lawyer to the provinces, as a tourist abroad (mostly in Paris), finally again to Petersburg where he watches the Revolution of 1917 and becomes one of its victims. He is a most interesting summary of the bourgeois intelligentsia in its process of Hamlet-like doubts and disintegration. We watch how, step by step, everything goes to seed in that particular circle : family, love, sex, culture, literature, politics, while the happenings in Russia seem to go on as though urged by an irresistible logic of their own. The final issue is, in fact, Intelligentsia and the Revolution. It is an answer, or at least Gorky's answer, to the question why the intelligentsia was so cruelly eliminated by the cataclysm of 1917.

VIII

EVEN A BRIEF SURVEY SUCH AS THIS SHOULD NOT OMIT mentioning Gorky's pamphlets, diaries, articles, essays, and especially his excellent reminiscences of Tolstoy, Korolenko, Chekhov, and Andreyev. Those of Tolstoy are among the shrewdest things ever written about that complicated genius. As though emulating Leskov, Gorky gives us here not analysis, but only a string of anecdotes and impressions, organised in such a manner as to present Tolstoy without the slightest hagiographical touch—intensely human and intensely alive.

Last but not least, Gorky was the initiator and the first theoretician of socialist realism, which is at present the most powerful current in the literature of Soviet Russia. This current does not imply any socialist propaganda as a kind of duty on the part of the writers. It simply means that in contrast to the pessimistic, negatively critical or else escapist literatures of the West, Soviet literature is imbued with a constructive faith (in this case a socialist one) aiming at eventual integration not only of the individual and society, but also of literature and life. In Gorky's opinion socialist realism "presents Being as action, as creation aimed at the unbroken development of the finest individual traits of man, that he may triumph over the forces of nature, that he may realise the joy of living on earth, which by his ever-increasing requirements he is induced to transform into a splendid place for all mankind united into a single family."

This active type of realism in the name of a new man and a new life involves by its very nature what might be called socialist humanism, which indeed is closely connected with Gorky's name. A society founded on the struggles and the hatred of classes necessarily requires countless victims and personal frustrations, by virtue of which the individual willy-nilly regards himself as an enemy of society. This feeling of hostility and general uprootedness grows, and so does the callous and destructive brand of pessimism. As Gorky himself pointed out, "in the twentieth century pessimism degenerated into a philosophy of complete social cynicism, into a complete and decisive denial of 'humanitarianism' of which in former times the bourgeois of all countries boasted so much." He saw the only remedy in a society based on a pattern which would form a synthesis of socialism and humanism. A synthesis of this kind is one of the great problems of today and of tomorrow. Here literature, as Gorky saw it, can be a powerful corrective. This is why, only two years before his death, he said in one of his talks : "I want literature to rise above reality and to look down on reality from above, because literature has a far greater purpose than merely to reflect reality. It is not enough to depict already existing things—we must also bear in mind the things we desire and the things which are possible of achievement."

IX

THIS LAST SENTENCE COULD BE USED AS A MOTTO FOR Gorky's work as a whole. In a number of his writings he proved to be the very embodiment of socialist humanism with its respect for human personality—not isolated and self-centred personality, but one directed towards, and consciously working for, its integration with society. No wonder that he became the idol of the new readers as well as the new intellectuals from among the Russian working classes, whose tastes and requirements differ considerably from those of the former intelligentsia. So we must not grumble if Soviet literature has not produced great authors comparable with Pushkin, Tolstoy, Dostoevsky, or Chekhov. Its task of clearing the ground for something new and perhaps constructive is not yet finished, however much it has already strengthened its own position and at the same time helped to level up the literary taste of the masses.

The success of this trend in particular can be judged

by the astronomical sales in the Soviet Union of the best Russian authors—from Pushkin onwards. According to the *Literary Gazette* (June 15th, 1946) Gorky's works alone have appeared, between 1917 and 1946, in sixty-six languages and have sold in 42,000,000 copies. It is doubtful whether any author anywhere else on earth could even dream of such sales. But a fact such as this also proves that the years which have passed since Gorky's death in 1936 have not impaired his stature. Having come from the people, he became the people's author in the truest sense of this word. And lastly, his own will and vitality seem to be symbolic of a nation which has shrunk from no labours, no sacrifices, and even no mistakes in order to shape the future according to its own vision of a better and nobler life on earth.

ELEVEN

Leonid Andreyev

I

IN EACH LITERATURE THERE ARE AUTHORS THE symptomatic significance of whose works is often greater than their artistic value. Typical not so much of their own epoch as a whole but rather of some of its conspicuous single facets, they are usually overrated during their life-time, and underestimated once they are dead. Such, at any rate, was the fate of Leonid Andreyev (1871-1919) who, between 1902 and 1910, was one of the most discussed writers in Russia and who, for a time, rivalled in popularity even Gorky himself. Nor is it without interest that the first literary successes of Andreyev were partly connected with Gorky's name, although he later became the antithesis of everything Maxim Gorky stood for. While Gorky worked for a new era, a new community and a new set of readers, Andreyev preferred to hitch his talent to the decaying bourgeois intelligentsia in order to reflect, as in a magnifying and also somewhat crooked mirror, their consciousness during the last few years before their passing out of history. Roughly from the middle of the 'nineties onwards, the spirit of despondence was being gradually replaced by the more hopeful moods, at least on the part of those intellectuals who saw the *raison d'être* of their existence in paving the way for a final clash with the forces of reaction. But when, in 1905, the clash took place, the reaction won a victory at once so brutal and so complete that most of the bellicose intellectuals were hurled, once again, into the slough of despond ; into a vacuum, where the demand for all kinds of dopes and escapes—aesthetic, "mystical," or even grossly sensuous—was on the increase. Andreyev seized the opportunity and became, overnight as it were, one of the most successful authors in Russia. But he was not the only one ministering to those particular needs of the defeated and defeatist intelligentsia. There were other modernists who, on different levels, played a similar part: Sologub, for instance, or Artsybashev.

Fyodor Sologub, a "highbrow" decadent and symbolist, differed from the rest in so far as he did not cater for popularity. Keeping away from public life, he shut himself in his private ivory tower, where he indulged in an aesthetic or would-be aesthetic cult of death and of weird necromantic phantoms. But even before reaching that stage, he had made—in his novel *A Petty Demon*—a formidable onslaught on that philistine vulgarity, the fight with which was considered almost a duty by every Russian author from

Gogol onwards. The hero of Sologub's novel—a paranoiac schoolmaster—outstrips even Gogol's worst examples of intensified vulgarity and, like the characters in *Dead Souls*, he is symbolic in his realism. But whereas Sologub cared for the elite, Artsybashev wrote for the rank and file of the demoralised intelligentsia ; for those in fact who were on the look-out for cheaper means of escape, even if this meant a surrender to sexual looseness, such as is preached in Artsybashev's sensational novel *Sanin*. He must have cashed in well on it, yet even in the heyday of his popularity (or notoriety) his success could not compare with that of Andreyev whose work falls, roughly, somewhere between that of Sologub and Artsybashev.

Apart from his early stories, the majority of Andreyev's writings deal with rather "big" subjects, treated in that hasty quasi-modernist style which, for all its pretentious garb, is generally accessible and therefore likely to flatter the vanity of the less tutored readers by giving them the illusion of being "high-brows." But this alone would hardly have brought him to the pinnacle of fame and prosperity, had he not sponsored some of those sensational themes which were bound to appeal to the intellectuals of the post-1905 period.

II

AS A SON OF A PETTY OFFICIAL IN THE PROVINCES Andreyev could not boast of a background spacious and cultured enough to give him that sureness of taste without the guidance (whether conscious or unconscious) of which even a great literary talent is likely to go astray in an age so full of experiments and vagaries as the one he lived in. On finishing his University studies, he became a lawyer's assistant—a profession he gave up when he discovered (from 1897 onwards) that he could make a living as an author. In his early stories the echoes of Chekhov, Korolenko and Gorky are noticeable. Soon the influences of Dostoevsky and Tolstoy were added, and later also that of Edgar Allan Poe. The writings of his early period are realistic, with a social or humanitarian undercurrent, but invariably ending in a minor key. The final note of his *Little Angel* (1899), for instance, is one of gloom and disillusionment. So is the ending of *Petka in the Country* (1899)—a pathetic story of a boy of ten slaving as a barber's assistant in Moscow, who for the first time in his life is taken for a holiday in the countryside ; but when his impressionable mind has opened to all the beauties of nature, he is forced to go back to his tedious drudgery in the Moscow slums.

Even when Andreyev became a member of Gorky's publishing firm *Znanie* (Knowledge), he made hardly any concessions to the social or humanitarian optimism of that group. One of such concessions is his story *In the Basement,* obviously implying—like Gorky's *Twenty-six Men and One Girl*—that even the hearts of the "ex-humans" still retain some sparks of true humanity which may flare up if given a chance. Two of Andreyev's best early stories, *Once there Lived* (1901) and *In the Fog* (1902) were partly inspired by Tolstoy —the first by *The Death of Ivan Ilyich*, and the second by *The Kreutzer Sonata*. *Once there Lived* takes place in a clinic where there are several patients knowing that they are doomed, but the atmosphere of death is handled with Chekhov's technique and, what is more, with Chekhovian understatement — a rare thing in Andreyev's writings. A different propensity is noticeable in *In the Fog*. Here Andreyev tackled the tragedy of awakened sex in a schoolboy who has contracted venereal disease and eventually murders a prostitute and commits suicide. The story caused much uproar and can serve as a proof of the author's growing hankering for sensational themes, worked out in a dramatic (or melodramatic) manner. This was particularly the case when he came under the spell of Dostoevsky's themes and problems. As the latter were often much bigger than his talent, he tried to make up for it by raising his tone and filling his pages with would-be symbolistic *clichés*, designed to surprise, or rather to stun his readers by means of an emphasis, propped up by paradoxical logic. This brought, however, a forced, not to say false note into his writings, and its falseness increased in the ratio in which he abandoned the straightforward realistic method for the sake of stilted pseudo-symbolism. This genre was clearly anticipated in stories such as *Silence*, *The Wall*, *The Tocsin*, *The Abyss*, and *The Thought* —all of them written between 1900 and 1902 in a mood of futility. Chekhov's pathetic blind-alley was taken up by Andreyev with relish, but he turned it into a substitute for religion, with its theology of "mystical anarchism," its solemnly hollow rites and incantations, the only genuine element in which was his fear of life. The apotheosis of this fear became Andreyev's "purpose" (one could almost say—moral purpose) which he piously cultivated as the very height of aesthetic modernism.

Always an individualist, Andreyev was strongly attracted by the heroic pose of a modern anti-philistine. But as he felt more and more the fascination of Dostoevsky's metaphysical rebels, he too became one of them without even believing in metaphysics. He prostrated himself before the principle of negation which he pushed to the verge of grotesqueness. Like some of Dostoevsky's heroes he saw (or forced himself to see) in life only a "vaudeville of the devils;" but instead of searching for something beyond it, as Dostoevsky did, he derived from the very hopelessness of such a disposition—into which he often worked himself up by means of alcohol—a peculiar and almost ecstatic pleasure.

III

ONE OF HIS FIRST SUCCESSFUL LONGER STORIES, IMBUED with such a nihilistic "purpose," was *Life of Father Vasily Fiveysky* (1903). The problem here tackled is the eternal problem of evil, only the questioner in Andreyev's story is a village priest whose unconditional faith in God is being gradually undermined by the horrors of life he sees around. Like a modern Job, Father Vasily passes through a series of personal and family misfortunes, including the birth of an idiot son. He first looks for comfort in the Christian faith, but his reiterations of the formula, "I believe, O Lord, I believe," are answered only by the imbecile laughter of his stinking little idiot and by an increase of evil—personal and otherwise. Outraged in his moral sense of justice, the priest hurls at last a mad challenge to God, but here he himself is crushed by the weight of the emptiness in a Godless and senseless world.

Senselessness is further stressed in Andreyev's story, *Phantoms* (1904)—obviously a literary descendant of Chekhov's *Ward No.* 6, with the action taking place in a lunatic asylum. The author analyses the imaginary phantom existence of the inmates in whose minds the boundary line between the normal and the abnormal has been obliterated. But life outside the asylum (especially in the fashionable night-club, where the doctor in charge spends most of his free time) is implied to be equally phantom-like ; so there is not much to choose. Or take *The Red Laugh* (1905)—a crudely pretentious monologue of an officer who lost both legs in the Russo-Japanese War, the "madness and horror" of which continue to haunt him in his invalid bed at home. In Andreyev's allegorical narrative, *Thus Was It and Will Be* (1905), the futility of revolutionary upheavals is marked by the clock of time and its indifference to the happenings on earth, the history of which remains the same bloodstained farce, no matter what antics and atrocities may be performed by the human Yahoos. With no less emphasis Andreyev stresses in another story, *My Memoirs* (1908), the nothingness of freedom and —by implication—of the fight for freedom. To crown it all, his turgid *Lazarus* (1906) brings such a nihilistic attitude to a head. Lazarus, resurrected by Christ, is more like a walking corpse, paralysing all the living with whom he comes into contact and reminding them by the mystery peering out of his eyes that life itself is only a form of death.

Yet if his "metaphysical" themes often outstrip his talent, Andreyev fares much better when concentrating mainly on psychology. One of his best stories of this kind, *The Governor* (1905), is told with restraint and with almost Tolstoyan matter-of-factness. The hero of the story is the governor of a province who in the turmoil of the revolution ordered that a gathering of workers should be shot at. As a consequence he receives an intimation from the local terrorists that they have sentenced him to death, and the certainty of impending doom hangs over him like fate itself, until the inevitable happens. As psychologist Andreyev had learned a great deal from Dostoevsky. At his best he also succeeded in skilfully combining psychological observations with some deeper thought which added to the value of the story. In his *Christians* (1904), for example, he unmasks with unflagging irony the hypocritical character of our Christianity, seen from the angle of a prostitute who obstinately refuses to take a Christian oath, to the indignation of the no-less-prostituted but otherwise respectable and respected citizens—obviously a mark of Tolstoy's influence.

More involved in its subject-matter is the story, *Darkness* (1907). Once again, Andreyev attacks morality, but this time from an unexpected and in its own way supra-moral angle. A revolutionary terrorist, whose whole life has been one long struggle for freedom and justice, is hiding from the police. The circle of his pursuers has grown so narrow that the only refuge where he still feels relatively safe is a house of ill-fame. As he has never been in such a place before, he is staggered by the filth and degradation he finds there. In his struggle for a better world he had kept pure and never touched a woman. Now, too, he would have nothing to do with the prostitute in whose room he is hiding. But having guessed who he is, and feeling offended by his purity, she asks him rather impertinently what right he has to be moral while she and millions of other human beings are compelled to wallow in filth. The problem unexpectedly sinks into his mind and, step by step, produces a strange reaction. Unable to behave like a "saved" moral prig amidst so much squalor around him, he begins to feel uneasy about his own "white robes" until he is actually ashamed of them. In the end he becomes conscience-stricken on account of his chastity, in which state of mind he is impelled by a strangely twisted *moral* impulse to degrade himself, and to fall so low indeed that even the gendarmes, who at last get hold of him, are disgusted—without suspecting the actual cause of his "immorality."

IV

ANDREYEV CAN BE GOOD, EVEN EXCELLENT, ONLY when he is less preoccupied with his nihilistic outlook than with the story as such, provided he tells it without affectations. The two of his longer though widely different narratives of this kind are *Judas Iscariot and Others* (1907) and *The Seven that Were Hanged* (1908).

The first of them is rather ambitious not only because it is connected with the Gospel, but on account of the mysterious personality of Judas himself. What were the motives behind his betrayal of Jesus Christ, since greed alone is too paltry an explanation ? Did he want to protect Jesus, hoping that while in prison He would be beyond the reach of the infuriated Jews ? Or was he anxious that Jesus should fulfil His mission without vacillating and thus proclaim His own glory to the world ? Without bothering about any previous explanations of the motives, Andreyev took a provocative line of his own. To begin with, his Judas is something of a self-divided modern misanthropist whose double nature is marked by the very shape of his ugly head. Endowed with far greater intelligence and knowledge of life than all the other disciples put together, he is suspicious and cynically scornful of human beings. He does not think much of the noisy plebeian Peter or of the smugly virtuous John, let alone the weak-minded simpleton Thomas. But he knows how to conceal his spite, as well as his cruel wisdom, behind the mask of a clown. There is only one person before whom he bows unconditionally and with fanatical devotion, namely Jesus. Judas the cynic would not question for a moment the Master's moral and spiritual greatness. The point about which he felt sceptical though was the assertion of Jesus that He was the Son of God, since the clever doubter Judas could hardly presume the existence of a God behind such a senseless world. He was puzzled by it to the point of actually betraying Jesus Christ in order to arrive at some certainty at least with regard to this matter. For if God exists at all, He would not allow the scoundrels to triumph over His beloved Son, and a miracle was sure to happen, proclaiming the Saviour's glory to the world. But even if God does not exist, the Master's hour of trial might still become an hour of triumph, because the mob, callous though it was, could not but recognise in Him the noblest being that ever trod the earth.

The betrayal took place. Insults were piled on Jesus. He was ridiculed, maltreated, tortured, spat upon, yet God remained silent: no miracle happened. And the howling mob, which not long before had shouted Hosanna in the streets of Jerusalem, now clamoured for the malefactor Barabbas to be set free instead of Jesus. During the Master's agony Judas, too, went through a crucifixion of his own. With anguish past endurance he watched the last hours of Jesus at a time when all the other disciples, prudently hiding, were able—to Judas's disgust—to eat and even to sleep. But of what account were the disciples now that everything had crumbled to pieces! The only thing left was to fling the money back into the faces of the pompous worthies responsible for the Master's fate and then clear out of a world in which such things were possible. Which he did.

The Seven that Were Hanged is much more topical. It was written during the worst days of the Stolypin regime, when hangings of the revolutionaries were a daily occurrence. Andreyev obviously wanted to join Tolstoy and Korolenko in their vigorous protest, only instead of a pamphlet he presented the world with a gruesome and in its own way intensely moving story about seven people—five revolutionaries and two ordinary criminals—condemned to die on the gallows. The thoughts, moods and emotions of each of them, from the sentence of death to the moment of their execution, are described with powerful directness and with warmth, although even here Andreyev is interested in the revolutionary personalities rather than in the revolution as such. Anyway, this time he paid due tribute to the fighters who sacrificed their lives for the sake of that better world about which he himself was so sceptical.

The dilemma of a selfless terrorist forms the backbone of Andreyev's only full-size novel, *Sashka Zhegulyov* (1911). Sashka is a young intellectual who, in the years of upheaval, joins the revolution from sheer altruism. He forms a band of terrorists, but in their practice criminal and revolutionary motives become so intermixed that in the end it is impossible to tell one from the other. Under duress the band dissolves, while its few remaining members are surrounded and killed. The novel bears the mark of Andreyev's weakening talent. The same can be said with greater justice about his *Satan's Diary* (1917), even if its idea of the devil (embodied in an American multi-millionaire) being out-deviled by human malice and baseness is not bad at all. As though feeling that his narrative zest was subsiding, Andreyev turned, from 1908 onwards, more and more to the theatre and the drama.

V

HE BEGAN WRITING PLAYS AFTER THE SUCCESS OF Maxim Gorky's *Lower Depths*. As he was at that time considered—in popularity at least—a rival of Gorky, it was natural that he should have emulated him also on the stage where he soon became more prolific than Gorky himself. From 1912 onwards he wrote practically nothing but plays. Like his stories, these can be divided into a realistic and a philosophic group, with the addition of a few pot-boilers of the kind that are sure to please the public. And like his stories again, they all reflect Andreyev's problem-hunting and nihilism *à outrance*.

In his first dramatic work, *To the Stars* (1905), he tackled the Nietzschean problem of one's love for the "far ones" as being something incompatible with the love for one's neighbours. His realistic *Savva* and his abstractly "expressionist" morality-play, *The Life of Man* (both written in 1906), testify to an even greater despair over man and life than his stories. "I survey with my eyes the earth," says Savva, "and I see that there is nothing more terrible than man's life." *Savva* is soaked in that negative revolutionary mood which wants to destroy mainly for the sake of destruction. Since history and civilisation have proved such a flop, then the best we can do is to scrap the whole of it and start afresh—perhaps with more success. Also the drama, *King Hunger*, is revolutionary in its protest against the capitalistic minority. The enslaved workers who rebel are crushed by the technocratic (or for that matter—"managerial") elite, but the muffled threats of the slain to come back do not augur well for the future of that elite. On the whole, this is one of Andreyev's weakest plays. As in *The Life of Man*, or even more so, he mistakes here allegory for symbolism, especially in the last scene the forced artificiality of which is positively painful.

In *The Black Masks* (1908) the Dostoevskian theme of self-divided personality crops up once more—this time in the shape of a "surrealist" nightmare, taking place in a brain already in the grip of madness. *Anathema* (1909), on the other hand, belongs to the more "titanic" genre. It is a pretentious allegorical melodrama on a Faustian scale, with all the faults of Andreyev the author underlined. Vaguely allegorical is also *He Who Gets Slapped* (1915). Here a former intellectual luminary has become a circus clown, celebrated on account of the prodigious number of slaps he is able to endure. Intellect itself (in the garb of a clown) lustily slapped in a circus to the delight of a gaping mob—such is the ulterior allegorical meaning of this otherwise realistic melodrama.

Among Andreyev's plays intended for the public at large the two pot-boilers, *The Days of our Life* (1908) and *Gaudeamus* (1910), about the life of the students, were great box-office successes. In the much more spicy *Anfissa* (1909), he piled up certain morbid elements, including incest, to the extent of verging on a naturalistic parody. *Katerina Ivanovna* (1912), *Professor Storitsin*, and *Thou Shalt not Kill* (1913) record the low and vulgar mentality of an epoch in which there is little room for the values of a higher order. A new departure in the direction of humorous satire was Andreyev's play, *The Pretty Sabine Woman* (1912)—a somewhat heavy skit on the opportunism of the Russian liberals of the period. One of Andreyev's last plays, *Samson in Chains*, tackles once again the drama of self-division, though more convincingly than in *The Black Masks*.

During the first World War Andreyev, for all his previous nihilism, suddenly became a patriotic bourgeois liberal and, after the Revolution of 1917, developed a violent hatred of the Bolsheviks. About two years later he died in his lonely villa in Finland. But had he lived longer, he could not have added anything to what he had said. As a mouthpiece of that layer of the intelligentsia which was already decayed to the extent of revelling in its blind-alley, and even in the prospect of its own historical death—waiting round the corner, he could not but share their fate, once the old order was swept away by the Revolution. No modern author of his potential calibre has paid such a heavy price for success as Andreyev.

TWELVE

Alexander Blok

I

ONE OF THE STRIKING FEATURES OF MODERN RUSSIAN literature is its alternation between poetry and prose. The Pushkin period, for example, was essentially one of poetry. Then from the 'forties to the beginning of the 'eighties monumental prose prevailed. But in the 'nineties a wave of modernist verse set in and reached its climax in Russian symbolism proper (notably in the work of Vyacheslav Ivanov, Andrey Bely, and Alexander Blok) during the first decade of this century. The early stage of this trend was frankly "decadent." Its appeal lay in an excessive "art for art's sake" attitude on the one hand, and in an exaggerated egotism—taken for the most part from Nietzsche—on the other. Its ingredients were similar to those in the "decadent" currents in Western Europe from which they had been largely derived. In Russia the escapist "ivory towers" of aestheticism and neoromanticism were, perhaps, even more tempting than anywhere else, since her political realities were often too unpleasant to be faced, let alone endured. Yet as creators of a new compensatory reality in the realm of fancy and beauty the modernist poets prided themselves on their exclusiveness, on being different from ordinary mortals, and were therefore anxious to write not for the crowd but for the elect. The gap between the "high-brow" reader and the mass reader thus could not be avoided. Certain aspects of the modernist movement actually demanded too great an artistic and literary culture to be accessible to all, for which reason they appealed the more to cliques and exclusive circles.

This led to sterile sectarianism and to an equally sterile detachment from life. Once aware of this, several Russian modernists began to champion a more vital conception of poetry which, instead of turning away from reality, would provide a deeper interpretation as well as affirmation of life. Efforts of this kind had to pass through numerous literary and philosophic ventures before they crystallised, during the first decade of the present century, into a definite school of Russian symbolism—as distinct from French symbolism, for example, which was concerned above all with the new methods of poetic expression. The principal Russian symbolists, while accepting those methods, were anxious to go beyond "mere" literature and were keenly interested in the genesis of a new consciousness, of a new man. Such speculations brought them, however, into contact with the writings of Dostoevsky and with those of Vladimir Solovyov.

Solovyov was the most conspicuous figure in the religious-philosophic thought of Russia towards the end of the last century. His aim was to work out an active synthesis of philosophy, religion, art and life. He dreamed of a universal regeneration of man and the world through Love (in a religious sense) as well as through that "integral fulness of existence" in which he saw the only alternative to universal anarchy and chaos. Unfortunately, he was not immune from the fallacies of those romantics who, instead of unifying such elements as thought, emotion, science, philosophy and religion, only mixed them and blurred the boundaries between them. Deeply versed in European and Eastern thought, in the teaching of the gnostics, as well as in Christian mysticism, Solovyov was both a philosopher and a poet. To his belief that " all transient things are but symbols" he added his vision of a new man and a new earth, and may therefore justly be called the first important representative of Russian symbolism proper. He partly anticipated it in a poem affirming that—

All that about us lies
Is but the shade, the mirrored image,
Of things not seen with eyes.

It was such an attitude towards the world that served as the starting point for the greatest and in his own way the most tragic figure in Russian symbolism—Alexander Blok (1880-1921).

ALEXANDER BLOK

II

IT SOUNDS LIKE A PARADOX THAT BLOK HAD VERY vague ideas of modern poetry before he was eighteen. The favourite authors of his youth were the dreamy Zhukovsky and those German romantics with whom he felt a certain affinity. It may have been due to their influence that his own early poems were imbued with a hazy medieval flavour, while Solovyov's work was responsible for the trend and perhaps even for the final awakening of Blok's poetic genius. Like Solovyov, he accepted the immanent mystical "World-Soul" (or the gnostic "Sophia"—the feminine hypostasis of divinity) as the Eternal Feminine, from which he hoped for a transfiguration of all life with a fervour strong enough to blend his religious and his erotic impulses in one powerful flame. His awakened sex turned entirely within, to the symbols and phantoms of his poetic imagination. He not only imagined—he actually felt Love to be the key to the mystery of the Universe. What in an ordinary talent might have resulted in dreamy sentimental outpourings was thus transformed by Blok's genius into his first accomplished book—*Verses about the Lady Fair* (1905).

In these poems, typical of his early period (roughly between 1897 and 1904), Blok combined Solovyov's yearning for the miraculous with the erotic dreaminess of a Novalis, and the music of Shelley with the tenderness of Dante's *Vita Nuova*, while yet imparting to them a style and a texture entirely his own. Evocative in a musical and magical sense, many of them sound like ardent prayers of a troubadour extolling the Eternal Feminine, symbolised in his own vision of the Lady Fair. But the distance between her and him is so immense that an approach is unthinkable. All he dare look forward to are a few fleeting moments in which her presence, with the glory of a different realm, would descend, like God's grace, upon him. As if unaware of the world around, Blok sings—at this stage—like a man in a trance, or like a medium, whose very passivity increases his poetic intoxication. His images, for the most part vague, are yet imbued with an uncanny "aura," radiating in each line. His language may still be reminiscent of Solovyov, but the melody and the "touch" are his own. And as for the wealth of his rhythms, his new musical and prosodic devices, they are enough to drive frantic even the most experienced of translators.

The guardian spirit hovering over Blok's poetry of that period was Solovyov the visionary and the mystic, even if Blok's raptures were not always as innocent as they looked. The prayer-like tone of his early poems (he wrote about eight hundred of them before he was twenty-five) was often disturbed by flashes of the opposite depth: that of spiritual descent, blasphemy and rebellion. This ambivalent element assumed for a while the form of fear, of ominous forebodings.

I am afraid of my double-faced soul,
And I carefully conceal
My diabolical and wild face
Underneath this sacred armour.

The awareness of the danger made him cling all the more to his mystical Beatrice. But he knew that descent was imperative, even inevitable in so far as he realised that he had no right to serve his ideal apart and away from life. And since he, too, was a man and not a ghost, he could not but wonder what would become of his vision on the plane of life as it is and not as it presents itself to a poet's imagination. His misgivings came out in this poem addressed at one of such moments to his Lady Fair:

I have foreknown Thee! Oh, I have foreknown Thee. Going
The years have shown me Thy premonitory face,
Intolerably clear, the farthest sky is glowing,
I wait in silence Thy withheld and worshipped grace!
The farthest sky is glowing: white for Thy appearing,
Yet terror clings to me: Thy image will be strange,
And insolent suspicion will arouse upon thy nearing,
The features long foreknown, beheld at last will change.
How shall I then be fallen!—low with no defender:
Dead dreams will conquer me, the glory, glimpsed will change,
The farthest sky is glowing! nearer looms the splendour,
*Yet terror clings to me. Thy image will be strange.**

III

WHAT HAPPENED BEFORE LONG WAS A COMPLETE change of "her" image. Having heard the summons

* Translated by Babette Deutsch and Avrahm Yarmolinsky in *Modern Russian Anthology* (Harcourt, Brace & Co. M. Lawrence).

of life, he had no right to ignore it. But once he had abandoned the realm of idealistic heights, he had to be ready for any shock in the realm of facts. To follow this second period (1904-07) means to watch the first act of the tragedy between Blok the man and Blok the poet, when his spiritual maximalism of "all or nothing" came into collision with the world as it is. In a somewhat flowery essay written in 1910 (i.e. during the growing crisis of Russian symbolism), Blok gave a veiled explanation of what had taken place. He deals in it with his inner experiences only. As these are treated in terms of his poetic activities on the one hand, and of life around on the other, he touches upon the problem of Art and Life in some of its acutest aspects, but, of course, from an entirely personal angle. On the plane of concrete earthly love and earthly existence there certainly was no room for such a symbol as the Eternal Feminine. Here his Beatrice was a romantic phantom, a myth, which, instead of bridging the gap between the actual and the transcendental, only widened it. The two worlds—the world of spiritual values and visions, and the world of facts—proved incompatible. One seemed to exclude the other. There was even no guarantee that his previous ecstasies had not been mere indulgence in subjective fancies rather than a gift of intuition with a higher reality behind it.

In this state of doubt and bewilderment, Blok was assailed by a swarm of "doubles" which had been dormant in him as an antithesis to his former aspirations. A further disappointment may have been due to his married life, from which he probably expected miracles that never happen.* Be this as it may, he found himself cut off from the "streaming light" of those regions where his imagination had soared before. His Lady Fair became a ghost, a doll, and all turned into a tragi-comic puppet show in which he and his likes were but actors and buffoons, whether they knew it or not. "Had I made a picture," he confesses in the essay mentioned, "I would have depicted it in this manner: in the lilac dusk of an endless world there sways an enormous white catafalque, and on it lies a doll whose face is dimly reminiscent of the countenance which once had shone through the heavenly dawns. . . . And so all is finished: my miraculous world has turned into an arena of my personal acting—into a puppet show in which I myself am only one of the company of my strange puppets. In other words, my own life has become art. . . . I stand before it all without knowing what to do either with the show, or with my life turned into art; for in my immediate presence there lives my own phantom-creation: neither alive nor dead—a blue ghost. . . . It is here that arises the problem of the curse of art, of a return to life, of service to the community."

This dilemma was typical of a man who, having lost his former romantic faith, still preserved his romantic temperament, which now began to play havoc with him. When such an incurable idealist is faced with the facts and conditions of real life, he cannot but react to them in Blok's manner. Romantic

* His wife Lyubov was the daughter of the famous scientist Mendeleyev.

irony and indictment play the principal part in it as they did in Blok's poetry which, from now on, became a strange psychological document and a confession—a record of his own inner drama. His lyrical play, *The Puppet Show* (*Balaganchik*, 1905), was one of the first attempts to ridicule his former visionary phase by means of buffoonery. From the angle of life as it is, the whole of that phase now appeared to him a tragic farce. And if his Lady Fair was but a doll or a ghost, then his own acts of devotion, as well as those of similar romantic Pierrots, were no more real than the gestures of puppets made of cardboard. In another little play, *The Stranger* (*Neznakomka*), he lets his Beatrice—symbolised as a star—fall down on to our earth, where she becomes an ordinary prostitute. Romantic irony thus passed into romantic blasphemy. But the old nostalgia was there and it still pursued him in haunting visions. In a poem under the same title, *The Stranger*, Blok wants to forget "her" by means of alcohol, but "she" hovers around him even in the dingy surburban restaurants, where every night—

At a certain hour infallibly,
(Or is this but a dream of mine?)
A girlish shape in silken draperies,
In the dark window seems to shine.

Always slowly and companionless,
Through drunken crowds she is seen to glide,
And in a cloud of fragrant loveliness,
She sits down at the window's side.

Spellbound by her presence, her shape, even by the nodding ostrich feathers in her hat, the poet is transferred for a moment to the hazy "magical shore" of the world he had been familiar with. And as his own drunkenness increases, he is ready to believe in the truth and reality of that world, knowing full well that this illusion, too, will disappear once the effect of wine is over.

Now I am lord of deepest mysteries,
The sun of another world is mine,
My soul is glowing with its radiance,
Filled with the bitter spirit of wine.

The ostrich feathers nodding dreamily,
Sway in my heart for evermore,
Those fathomless blue eyes are flowering
Upon a wondrous distant shore.

In my soul there's hidden a treasury,
It has one key—the key is mine,
Yes, you are right, tipsy monstrosities—
*Now I know, there is truth in wine.**

Having become something of a Don Juan, Blok looked in his love-adventures, too, as he did in wine, for an escape from the drabness of existence. But even in the hectic love poems, in which he sings of the real women who had loved him, there vibrates the repressed nostalgia for his vanished Beatrice:

* Translated by V. de Sola Pinto. In the original the first and third lines are also rhymed.

Yes, I have loved. And the mad glowing
Of love's drunk pain is at an end,
The triumph and the overthrowing,
The name of "foe," the word of "friend."

There have been many . . . are all fleeting?
Mere memories and shades of dreams,
Strangely I call them up, repeating
The golden music of their names.

There have been many, but a single
Charm bound them all in unity,
One frenzied Beauty made them mingle:
*Its name is Love and Life to me.**

IV

AWARE OF HIS "PUPPET SHOW," BLOK WAS NOW READY to face reality, while yet refusing any compromise with it. The "respectable" normal course of existence was outside his ambitions; worse—outside his taste. Life meant to him above all intensity of experience, intensity at any price. And when he could no longer procure it through the ecstasies of the heights, he plunged into those of the depths—into the emotional chaos of the Unconscious, of the "psychics," tinged with his own pessimism and tedium. But even on this level Blok could not continue without a substitute for his former Beatrice. He had to find a new beloved,

* Translated by C. M. Bowra in *A Book of Russian Verse* (Macmillan).

but a more tangible one, upon whom he could again project his yearnings, his faith, his passion for the boundless. This new beloved of his was now Russia—not the "holy" but the irrational Russia of endless spaces, winds and blizzards ; of flying *troikas* ; of maddening nostalgia, drunkenness and chaos.

I will listen to the voice of drunken Russia
And I will rest under a tavern roof.

Snow-Mask is the title of his most typical book of that period, and its main note is one of intoxication with the blizzards, with wine, with passion. The delight in self-annihilation rings in the accents of his sensual *Faina*. In the more virile verses of another section, *Enchantment through Fire*, his wish to come to terms with life flared up, but only for a moment. What followed was a new surrender to psychic drugs, but soon he could not rely on them ; he was compelled to look upon the world with a sobered mind and with more than sobered eyes.

The prevalent mood of that phase (from 1908 until 1917, that is, between the two Revolutions), can best be defined as spiteful apathy. The filth and the vulgarity of existence overpowered him to such an extent as to make all effort appear futile. The title of a collection of poems written in those years is itself significant—*The Loathsome World*. In *Iambi* he tried to kindle his crushed faith in life ; in his romantic drama in verse, *The Rose and the Cross* (1912), even his one-time devotion to the Lady Fair was revived. Yet the fire that was now burning came too much out of the ashes. The same can be said of his cycle *Carmen*, with its temporary outburst of carnal passion. The world seemed "loathsome" in all its aspects. But the more deeply he felt the futility of things the more intense became he as a poet. Having abandoned his trance-like vagueness and music, he adopted a vocabulary which was tersely realistic and at the same time symbolic. These two short poems, both of them written in 1912, convey his moods and his methods during that period. The theme is *Night in Petrograd.* And this is what Blok has to say about it:

Night : the street, a foolish lamp giving
A dingy light, a druggist's store :
For a quarter of a century go on living,
No escape. All will be as before.

You die: afresh you start life boldly,
Just as of old each detail repeat.
Night, the canal rippling so coldly,
*The druggist's store, the lamp, the street.**

In the second poem the condensed big-city nightmare is rendered as follows:

An empty street: light in a single window gleams.
The Jew apothecary is moaning as he dreams.

Before the cupboard labelled "poison" he can see,
Intently bending down on ghastly creaking knee

A skeleton wrapped in a cloak, who all the while
Searches for something, twists his black mouth in a smile.

* Translated by V. de Sola Pinto.

Finding it, he stumbles unaware and makes
A noise, then turns his death-head while the sleeper wakes,

Screams and rises in his bed, and falls on the other side,
But the visitor beneath his cloak can hide

The accursed phial for two noseless women there,
*Waiting outside beneath the street lamp's cold white glare.**

An even more typical example of Blok's symbolic realism is his *Danse macabre* which we quote in a paraphrased version (done by R. M. Hewitt):

It's hard for a corpse in this world of men,
Better remain apart, alone,
You have to mix with them now and then
Or you'll never succeed in your career.
But oh! the fear that they might hear,
The rattle of bone on bone.

Live men still sleep when the dead man rises.
His thoughts are black as the day is long,
Plods to the office, bank or assizes,
Where quills whisper a welcome-song.

Hour by hour must the dead man labour;
At last he's free and puts on his coat,
Wags his haunches, grins at his neighbour
And feeds him a bawdy anecdote.

The rain has smeared with a nameless liquor
Houses and churches and humans grimy;
But the dead man drives where the mud is thicker,
Knowing a place that is still more slimy.

* Translated by V. de Sola Pinto.

A gilded hall with mirrors about it.
Imbecile hostess and husband fool
Are glad to see him, who can doubt it?—
His evening suit was made by Poole.

Corpse, be brave now, raise thanksgiving:
They can't hear the rattle against that band:
No easy work to prove you are living,
But go round briskly, shake their hand.

Who is that by the distant column?
His eyes light up, for she too is dead,
Under their patter, with faces solemn,
Words that are real words are said.

"*Weary friend, I am lost and strange here.*"
"*Weary friend, I've nothing to tell,*"
"*It's midnight now.*" "*Oh, there's no danger—*
Dance with my niece, she likes you well."

And over there with senses reeling,
Waiting alert, her blood on fire,
The virgin stands, her eyes revealing
The ecstasy of life's desire.

With fluent malice more than human,
He murmurs into her ear alone,
Just as a live man woos a woman.
"*How clever he is, how kind and dear!*"
But somewhere near she can faintly hear
The rattle of bone on bone.

Another longer poem (or rather a cycle of poems), *The Life of My Friend*, is written in the same vein.

In his beautiful *Garden of Nightingales* Blok the dreamer emerged again with all the magic of his verbal art, but one of his recurring motifs during the whole of that period was his thought and his love of Russia. When everything else had disappointed and betrayed him; when he was tormented by forebodings about the "cold and gloom of the days to come," his love for Russia never faltered, although he was profoundly aware of her failings, enumerated in a poem which begins (1914):

To sin unashamed, to lose, unthinking,
The count of careless nights and days,
And then, while the head aches with drinking,
Steal to God's house, with eyes that glaze. . . .

There follows a long list of vices and transgressions, depicted in all their ungainliness. But as if aware of something different and deeper underneath it all, Blok exclaims in the end:

Dearer to me than every other,
*Are you, Russia, even so.**

V

THE MIXTURE OF DISGUST AND DESPAIR, SO MUCH IN tune with the atmosphere which followed the abortive revolution of 1905, was only the reverse side of Blok's

* Translated by Babette Deutsch and Avrahm Yarmolinsky in *Russian Poetry* (M. Lawrence).

suppressed idealism, of his yearning for a total change of man and life. This yearning was shattered in him, now and then, but never destroyed; which explains his secret hopes that an elemental catastrophe would come at last and cleanse the earth of its quagmire. His hopes turned into prophetic forebodings and even into certainty, especially with regard to Russia. These he uttered in a number of poems (*On the Field of Kulikovo*, *The Voice from a Chorus*, etc.), one of which, *Russia in* 1914, deserves to be quoted in full.

They do not remember the paths they have taken,
These children of a peaceful hour:
We are born of a Russia by terror shaken—
To forget the past is not in our power.

O years that crumble away into ashes,
Bringing madness or hope's bright dreams?
From freedom's flame or war's dire flashes
A blood-red light on men's faces gleams.

Dumbness—and then the tocsin ringing:
Each mouth is sealed and so we wait;
In hearts that once with joy were singing,
There's now an emptiness charged with fate.

And when the crows in the sky shall hover,
Above us lying beneath the sod,
May there be better men to look over
*This Thy kingdom, O God, O God.**

Only an attitude such as this can explain why Blok was one of the first to greet the Revolution of 1917 with

* Translated by V. de Sola Pinto.

demands and expectations of his own. At last the gap between his "art" and the "service to community" was likely to disappear so far as he was concerned. He sensed a deep symbolic meaning even in the horrors of those years: it was a new Apocalypse in the very compass and intensity of which there was hope. Far from being perturbed by it, he identified it with that elemental "spirit of music" which—according to him—is at the bottom of all creative revolutions. What he actually meant by it was analogous to Nietzsche's "Dionysian spirit." Both Nietzsche and Blok saw the cause of the *one-sided* development of European mankind in our "Socratic" rationalism—severed from that irrational spring of life which Nietzsche labelled with the name of Dionysos and Blok with the "spirit of music." The divorce between Reason and Nature as well as the Cosmos itself was, in their opinion, at the root of all the aberrations characteristic of modern man and civilisation. Having lost his sense of the irrational, the infinite, the timeless, man has been deprived of his true focus and narrowed down to his petty rationalism and even pettier egoistic concerns, without suspecting that life, real life begins only where such bondage ceases and the sway of the timeless "music of the universe" begins. This is how Blok explains it in his essay *The Downfall of Humanism* (1919):

"There are two kinds of time, one historical according to the calendar, and the other 'musical', without date or number. In the consciousness of civilised man the first kind alone is immutably present: but it is only when we realise how near we are to Nature, only when we abandon ourselves to the wave of music issuing from the chorus of the Universe, that we live in the second. For life in days, months and years no balance of our powers is necessary. And this absence of necessity for effort soon reduces the majority of civilised people to the state of mere dwellers upon the earth. But balance becomes indispensable as soon as we live near the 'musical' reality of the world—near to Nature, to the elemental. For this we need above all to be well-ordered both in body and spirit, since it is only with the complete body and the complete spirit acting together that the 'music of the universe' can be heard. Loss of balance between the bodily and the spiritual inevitably makes us lose that music. It makes us lose the ability to escape from the time of the calendar, that is, from historical days and years, into the other time that cannot be calculated. Epochs in which this balance is not destroyed may be called epochs of culture, in contrast to those when an integral perception of the world is beyond the bearers of an outlived culture, owing to the influx of melodies up to that time unfamiliar and unknown, which over-crowded the hearing. The influx may be slow if measured by the calendar, for new historical forces come into the consciousness of humanity gradually. Yet that which takes place slowly according to the laws of one kind of time can be completed suddenly according to the laws of the other. The movement of the one directing baton is enough to turn into a hurricane the drawn-out melody of the orchestra.

The mistake of the inheritors of humanistic culture, the fatal contradiction into which they fell, originated in their exhaustion. The spirit of integrity, the 'spirit of music,' abandoned them, and so they blindly put their trust in historical time. They failed to see that the world was already rising at a signal from a movement which was entirely new. While continuing to believe that the masses were acquiring freedom within the individualistic movement of civilisation, they naturally could not see that those very masses were bearers of a different, of a new, spirit."

The old romantic in Blok thus came out in his attitude towards the Revolution, but this time with a definite view about the creative value of the hurricane which brought into history, so dramatically, a "different new spirit." Carried away by the sway of this spirit, he felt a stirring of his hopes and of his poetic inspiration. It was in January, 1918, that is, during the cruellest civil war and havoc, that he wrote his *The Twelve* and *The Scythians*, both echoing the Revolution.

VI

THE FIRST OF THEM IS THE HIGH WATERMARK OF BLOK'S poetry. Incredibly simple yet full of ingenious rhythms and new devices (including phrases taken from the street and from the factory ditty), it seems to defy all attempts at an adequate translation. But even those who can read it in the original will miss a great deal if they fail to see in it a work in which all the ingredients of Blok's poetry meet as though in a knot. The romantic, the realist and the symbolist collaborate here on equal terms. So does his hatred of the old world ; his tedium and bitterness ; his love of the "mad" irrational Russia with her wind-swept spaces ; his revelling in the immensity of events ; and finally, his vision of a new world arising out of the chaos itself. The very opening reminds one of winds and blizzards in some of Blok's earlier poems :

Black dusk grows,
Snow falls white,
Wind, wind blows!
On his legs a man can't stand upright.

Wind, wind blows—
Through all creation the wind goes.

The wind twists and twirls
The white snow.
There is ice below ;
Heavy slippery—
If you try to go,
Down you fall—what a pity!

The wind reels, the snow dances ;
A party of twelve men advances.
Black rifle-slings upon their backs.
And flame, flame, flame upon their tracks.
With crumpled caps, lips smoking fags,
All should be branded as prison lags.

This is how the poet introduces the twelve Bolshevik guards, patrolling the streets of Petrograd, at night, during the Civil War and Revolution. The poem has twelve parts, each of them composed in a different rhythm and with different contents. The language is appropriate to the *dramatis personae* and the situation. It is the language of the street, interspersed with the revolutionary slogans and the talk of the twelve soldiers.

The narrative incident itself is crude and could have been taken from any police chronicle. One of the twelve patrolling soldiers, infatuated with the street-girl Katya (whose stockings are "packed with Kerensky notes") shoots her dead unintentionally —while aiming at his own rival in love. Throughout the poem we can follow his reactions to the crime, but this personal drama is cunningly interwoven with the chaos of a bleak northern winter and of the Revolution. The tension of the conflicting social strata is suggested by the rhythm, the tone and the accent of each verse, as well as by Blok's sallies against the old "bourgeois" order:

The bourgeois, where the roads divide,
Stands with his nose sunk in his fur ;
And, hairy, shivers at his side
With drooping tail, a poor whipped cur.

Like the dog, stands the bourgeois, hungry,
A silent question to the sky ;
The old world, like a homeless mongrel,
With tail between its legs stands by.

Nothing that belongs to the old world matters any longer. Even the "Holy Russia" of yore can be blasphemed, and, hooligan-fashion, trampled underfoot for the sake of a new era:

Don't shrink, comrade, get your rifle out;
Give Holy Russia a taste of shot.
At the wooden land,
Where the poor huts stand,
And her rump so grand!
Aha, but no Cross!

The fury of destruction, with "no Cross," fills the air. But however un-Christian its external ravages, a revolution in the name of justice and brotherhood is nevertheless based on a Christian impulse, which in the end must win—provided the revolution itself is imbued with that "spirit of universal music" of which Blok spoke in his essay. This is where the creative element of the revolution comes in, no matter whether the participants are aware of it or not. So "the twelve" (a distorted reflection of the twelve Apostles) march on. And in the midst of all the desolation, crime and chaos they are suddenly joined by an apparition which confers upon the poem a final message and meaning:

On they march with sovereign tread,
With a starving dog behind,
With a blood-red flag ahead—
In the storm where none can see,
From the rifle bullets free,

Gently walking on the snow,
Where like pearls the snowflakes glow,
Marches rose-crowned in the van
*Jesus Christ, the Son of Man.**

VII

The Twelve, NOW WORLD FAMOUS, IS PERVADED with the pathos of revolution and yet remains elusive enough to be interpreted in a number of ways. Christ as the leader of the twelve Bolshevik guards may appear to some people a blasphemy, to others a *deus ex machina* —the more so because nothing in the poem makes one expect such a denouement. On the other hand, He can be explained as a Messianic symbol of that creative side of the revolution which ought to follow upon the Inferno of suffering, blood and destruction. A revolution devoid of inner meaning remains only a calamity which has not been deepened into a purifying tragedy, and a mere calamity is always crushing and sterile. Blok knew that an event of such dimensions as the cataclysm of 1917 could not be without a meaning, and he said so. *The Twelve* was a final attempt on his part to regain his faith in humanity and in life—an attempt expressed in strains of which only great poetry is capable.

Less elusive and somewhat programmatic is his other poem, *The Scythians.* It was written during the

* Translated by C. M. Bowra in *Horizon* (July 1944).

peace negotiations at Brest-Litovsk and represents a platform counterpart to *The Twelve.* Here Blok challenges the luke-warm "bourgeois" West to join the universal brotherhood inaugurated by the Revolution, or else—to tremble before a barbaric invasion to come. In a spirit redolent of both the "populists" and the neo-Slavophils, he reproaches the Western nations as a revolutionary and as a Russian:

Yes, you have long since ceased to love
As our cold blood can love ; the taste
You have forgotten of a love
That burns like fire and like fire lays waste.

Yes, Russia is a Sphinx. Exulting, grieving,
And sweating blood, she cannot sate
Her eyes that gaze and gaze and gaze
At you with stone-lipped love for you, and hate.

This "stone-lipped love and hate" in one with regard to Europe forms another link between Blok and the Messianic Slavophil Dostoevsky. Only Blok's Messianism has nothing to do with the past—it is turned to a future growing out of the Revolution. Hence his appeal to the sceptical and reluctant West:

Come unto us, from the black ways of war,
Come to our peaceful arms and rest,
Comrades, while it is not too late,
Sheathe the sword ! May brotherhood be blessed.

And in case the Western nations should refuse to join, he threatens them with the "Asiatic face" of Russia, as well as with her indifference to their fate.

We will not move when the ferocious Hun
Despoils the corpse and leaves it bare,
Burns towns, herds cattle in the church
*And smell of white flesh roasting fills the air.**

Little did he suspect that the "smell of white flesh roasting" (in Belsen, etc.) would—in a few years—be practised not by the savage Asiatics, but by the "civilised" inhabitants of the heart of Europe. In the year of grace 1918 history was not yet "fantastic" enough to make such a supposition probable.

VIII

"LIFE IS ONLY WORTH LIVING WHEN WE MAKE IMMENSE demands upon it," Blok wrote (quite in the spirit of Gorky's socialist realism) in an essay at the time of his two revolutionary rhapsodies. "All or nothing! A faith, not in what is not found upon earth, but in what ought to be there, although at the present time it does not exist and may not come for quite a while." Approaching the Revolution with such an attitude, he saw its scope in nothing less than a gradual remaking of the world. "A true revolution cannot aim at anything less, though we cannot yet say whether this aim will be accomplished or not. Its cherished hope is to raise a universal cyclone which will carry to the

* Translated by Babette Deutsch and Avrahm Yarmolinsky in *Russian Poetry* (M. Lawrence).

lands buried in snow the warm winds and the fragrance of orange groves, and will water the sun-scorched plains of the south with the refreshing rain from the northern regions. *Peace and the brotherhood of nations* is the banner under which the Russian Revolution marches on its way. This is the tune of its roaring flood. This is the music which he who has ears to hear should hear."

Such was Blok's idea of the great "cyclone" which he, an intellectual, joined without hesitation. At the same time he turned bitterly against those members of the intelligentsia who had not followed his example (and they were the majority). His own maximalist demands made him impatient to see the economic and political upheaval completed by an adequate inner change in man himself, but the pace of this change was, and had to be, much slower than he expected. It must have been the discrepancy between the external and the inner revolutions—a discrepancy which assumed rather ugly aspects during the Civil War, the famine, and the Cheka—that eventually damped Blok's hope and enthusiasm.

Disappointment, apathy and illness closed upon him, and practically silenced him during the last two years of his life. He died in 1921, at the age of forty-one.

Blok's death coincided with the disintegration of that symbolist school in Russia of which he was the acknowledged leader. But quite apart from this, he was and still remains one of the most significant poets in the whole of modern Europe.

THIRTEEN

Sergey Esenin

I

RUSSIAN SYMBOLISM REACHED IN ALEXANDER BLOK not only its climax but also its crisis. A reaction against its vagueness and mistiness was therefore inevitable. It began soon after 1910 and took, on the whole, three directions. The so-called acmeist group, led by Gumilyov (executed in 1922), Anna Akhmatova and Sergey Gorodetsky, was all out for concreteness and clarity. The second group consisted of the futurists who, despite such gifted poets as Khlebnikov and Mayakovsky as their leaders, were at first looked upon too much as literary freaks to be taken seriously. More successful was the third group—that of stylised village poets who, in a way, lined up' their poetry to the work of Koltsov and Nekrasov. The earlier representative of this trend, Nikolai Klyuyev (1887-1926), was still connected with the symbolist school, and so was, for a while,

SERGEY ESENIN

Sergey Esenin (1895-1925). It was during the decay of that school that Esenin emerged on its fringes as one of the strongest and most promising young talents.

He on the one hand, and Mayakovsky on the other, are the two dominant figures among the crop of the poets who came into their own during the first decade of the Soviet regime. Yet what a contrast between these two gifted youths, both of whom ended eventually by suicide! While Mayakovsky became the poetic voice of the rising proletarians, Esenin preferred to turn his enormous gift into a lament for the old peasant Russia, and he could hardly have made any other choice. Born and brought up in the depths of rural Russia (the district of Ryazan), Esenin was so much steeped in the soil and the peasant lore that he was never able to detach himself from them, not even when he did his best to fit into the life of the capital, or into the spirit of the revolution. It would be a mistake, though, to regard his rural poetry from the angle of mere village folk-lore or local colour. It goes deeper. In a way it could be defined as poetic self-assertion of the "eternal peasant" against the encroaching machine and the mentality of the industrial town. The village in its primeval quintessence, sifted through his individual temperament, found in Esenin's verse one of the most poignant expressions in the whole of modern poetry. It was and remained the basic and perhaps the only source of his inspiration.

This modern village poetry assimilated quite a few technical devices from the symbolist movement. It even looked at first as though it would impart a new vitality to symbolism itself at a time when the latter was already on the decline. No wonder Klyuyev was so quickly promoted to the rank of an outstanding poet. A true Russian moujik, who yet remains at his shrewdest when pretending to be most humble and simple, Klyuyev is worth studying as a character. And he is certainly worth studying as a poet, since his verse bears the authentic stamp of the peasantry from whom he sprang. It was this current that reached its peak in Esenin whose path to fame began soon after his arrival in Petersburg in 1916.

Esenin, like Klyuyev, knew how to conceal at his debut a great deal of peasant cunning behind the pose of a "gentle shepherd swain," all of which was taken for the real thing by the Petersburg intelligentsia. His one-time friend, the poet Mariengof, tells us in a book about him that Esenin used to put on an embroidered blouse (the kind he may not have worn even while staying in the village), a peasant cap and top boots, after which he would play on the accordion village tunes—to the satisfaction of the highbrows who thus came into touch with the "people" without needing to leave their comfortable drawing rooms. Esenin, who had made good use of such comic-opera masquerades, probably chuckled at his audiences with no less amusement than the "little moujik" Klyuyev must have done during his own first steps towards fame. But apart from that, Esenin—like Klyuyev—was made of the stuff true poets are made of. Gorky goes so far as to proclaim him, in an article, the greatest lyrical genius since Pushkin. More authentic in his poems than in his peasant blouses, top boots and accordions, Esenin sang with a new accent born out of his very nostalgia for the cornfields he had left behind.

O fields of corn, O fields of corn,
An orphan's grief is mine ;
Heavy on my heart lies yesterday,
But in my heart you shine.

The fleeting miles whistle like birds
About my horse's mane
And the sun is sprinkling lavishly
Her holy healing rain.

O land of floods and agony
And gentle spring-tide powers,
Under the masters Dawn and Stars
I passed my schooling hours.

While in the Bible of the winds,
I pondered o'er the words,
Isaiah came and walked with me
*To keep my golden herds.**

Esenin's pastoral motifs, far from being a repetition of the hackneyed old melodies, vibrate with such freshness and sincerity that, in spite of his calculated experiments in poetic technique (new rhythms and forms), they sound as if extemporised. He often achieved surprisingly original texture and inflection

* Translated by R. M. Hewitt in *A Book of Russian Verse*, edited by C. M. Bowra (Macmillan).

by the manner in which he used peasant imagery and peasant idioms as one of his expedients. Religion, poetic superstition, naive animism and pantheism seem to vie with each other to make him produce that intimate yet strangely remote atmosphere which permeates the poems of his early period. But this was only one facet of Esenin's work. Its second and for a while hidden aspect was that potentially anarchic spirit of the steppes which, lurking in their unconscious, was perhaps more typical of the pre-revolutionary Russian peasants than were their seeming quietism and submissiveness. Whereas in the West the word freedom is associated with society, in Russia it used to be inseparable from the idea of the boundless spaces where everything seems to be on a bigger and more lavish scale than in Europe. This spirit in particular was responsible for their inner restlessness, as well as their frequent excess in everything : in piety and sacrilege, in meekness and cruelty, in active idealism and anarchic destruction. Esenin—an "essential" peasant from those spaces, stretching into the heart of Asia—actually confessed in one of his lyrics : "I cherish my secret purity of heart ; but still I may murder someone to the whistle of the autumn wind. . . ." It may be that the same unruly spirit rather than any convictions made him hail the revolution even while he, too, expected from the latter a renewal of life. The sentimental-idyllic and the turbulent elements were intertwined in him as in a fugue, out of which emerged some of his most remarkable melodies.

SERGEY ESENIN

II

UNHAMPERED BY EDUCATION OR EXCESSIVE READING, Esenin relied, like Nekrasov before him, on the sureness of his poetic instinct which made him glean the right kind of words, metaphors and images in the depths of the folk-genius itself. Most of his symbols, especially in his early poems, were connected with the archaic life of the village, and he enlarged them now and then —in a mythological sense—to cosmic dimensions. God and the saints are treated by him as something inseparable from the fields, the seasons, and the cattle. God is referred to as a grey elder sowing stars like winter corn. Esenin's landscape has the meek eyes of a cow. The dawn over the cornfields reminds him of a cow licking her newly born calf. The moon is a golden puppy, or else a "curly lamb gambolling in a blue meadow." He also knows how to combine his peasant vision with unexpected up-to-date similes and associations. One of his early poems consists of these four lines:

Where dawn is watering the cabbage rows,
Splashing red pails upon her mighty jamb,
A little nuzzling maple reaches up,
*To suck the full green udders of its dam.**

In another poem he compares the Russian autumn to a chestnut mare cleaning her "rough mane."

* This and the next two poems are taken from *Russian Poetry*, translated by Babette Deutsch and Avrahm Yarmolinsky (M. Lawrence).

Her hooves' blue clatter sounds above the bank,
Of the still river where the reeds are rank.
The monkish wind steps lightly, and retrieves
With idle fingers handfuls of dry leaves,
And where a rowan blooms he stoops to lean
And kiss the red wounds of a Christ unseen.

Or take these few characteristic lines :

In the clear cold the dales grow blue and tremble,
The iron hooves beat sharply ; knock and knock.
The faded grasses in wide skirt assemble
Flung copper where the wind-blown branches rock.
For empty straths, a slender arch ascending :
Fog curls upon the air and, moss-wise grows,
And evening, low above the wan streams bending,
In their white waters washes his blue toes.

The "essential" peasant was so strong in Esenin that he could not shed him even after he had turned to other themes and interests. While piling up laurels and disillusionments in the two Russian capitals, he still regarded the hut and the cornfields of his childhood as his only home. And when the revolution came, Esenin welcomed it in a spirit which was entirely different from that of Blok or Mayakovsky. He hailed it neither as a dissatisfied intellectual who thought he had found an outlet in the new Apocalypse ; nor as a proletarian, dancing on the ruins of the old world, but exclusively as a peasant and a villager. It was the turbulent yet Utopian villager in Esenin that made him write, in 1919, the revolutionary paean *Inonia* —a peasant counterpart to Blok's *The Twelve.*

SERGEY ESENIN

III

Inonia IS, TOGETHER WITH BLOK'S FAMOUS POEM, Klyuyev's *Lenin*, and Andrey Bely's *Christ is Risen*, among the most outspoken Messianic affirmations of the Russian Revolution on the part of the still lingering symbolists on the one hand, and the village poets on the other. Louder and more exuberant than *The Twelve*, Esenin's *Inonia* expresses the vision of a millennium ruled, not by the proletarians and their machines, but by the peasants inhabiting a free and universal Arcadia: quite in the style of those "populists" who once dreamed of a Russia untainted by the horrors of industrialism. Revolutionary in its tone and language, the poem thus seems to be anti-proletarian in its very subject.

If *The Twelve* can be likened to a disciplined and almost fettered ecstasy, *Inonia* is delirium passing into emotional and rhetorical debauch. As though intoxicated with his own words and visions, Esenin here lets loose not only his Utopian moods, but also his latent turbulence, verging on spiritual hooliganism. The result is a strange torrent of poetry and of verbal hysteria. "I will shear the blue firmament like a mangy sheep of its wool," he shouts almost with foam on his lips. "I will bite through the Milky Way. I will raise my arms as high as the Moon and will crack her like a nut. . . . With my firm hand I am ready to turn upside down the whole world. . . . Eight wings are splashing in stormy blizzards from my shoulders." And so on—one "colossal" simile hurled upon another. Forgetting the meek peasant Saviour of his former days, Esenin now yells in a raucous voice: "The body, the body of *Christ* I will spit out of my mouth." But what he offers instead is his vague Arcadian idyll "where the Deity of the living resides;" where there is faith in power, and Truth is to be found only in man himself. The worn old phrases, repeated in a new fortissimo.

This poem is a landmark between Esenin's early lyrics and his "imaginist" experiments, the limitations of which he recognised soon enough. Russian imaginism (analogous to, but not identical with, Anglo-American imagism) was ushered into existence in 1919 with a manifesto which proclaimed images the means as well as the aim of poetry, and therefore something self-sufficient to the extent of dispensing, when necessary, even with logic or coherence. In their search for original images, the adepts of this current often strained their fancy to the point of grotesque obscurity and distortion. Otherwise the movement hardly showed much vitality. But for the fact that Esenin happened to be one of its temporary members, it might have passed unnoticed, and even he cleared out of it before long. "Imaginism was a formal theory we wanted to affirm," he wrote in a subsequent autobiographical note, "but it had no ground under it and died, leaving the truth behind that only organic images are of value." But whether in or outside the group, Esenin had his fill of the excesses which bohemian and underworld Moscow of the NEP period could offer him.

SERGEY ESENIN

IV

ASSOCIATED WITH A FEW OTHER TURBULENT THOUGH less talented poets, Esenin must have felt strangely out of place in the turmoil of the Soviet capital. Yet he forced himself to fit into it and to satisfy at least the unruly element in him. He did all he could to beat the bohemians on their own ground, in which he seems to have succeeded. Jeeringly he walked about —his "head unkempt and like an oil lamp," glad to welcome any scandal, any escapade. Night brawls, prostitutes, taverns, police stations, hospitals, irresponsible marriages and divorces—such was his record of those riotous years. To make things worse, he met the famous dancer Isadora Duncan who, at the behest of the Soviet Government, came to Moscow in order to conduct a dancing school for children. Esenin, handsome and still in his prime, proved so irresistible that Isadora and he soon got married, both of them knowing full well how unsuitable they were for anything even remotely connected with married life.

The consequences could have been predicted. In due course Esenin grew tired and irritated. In his fits of retrospective jealousy he often treated his easy-going wife *à la moujik*, until a time came when the only thing to do was to part. But even this was not done without scenes, a glimpse into which is provided by this passage, taken from *Isadora Duncan's Russian Days* by Irma Duncan and Allan Ross Macdougall (Gollancz) : "Some time later, one afternoon when Isadora sat in her room with some callers Esenin came again to demand his bust. He demanded it loudly and instantly, and finally forced his drunken way into the room. The bust, which Konienkov had genially hacked out of a huge block of wood, stood atop a high bric-a-brac cabinet in one corner of the room. When Isadora refused to give him the bust and asked him to come back again some time when he was more fit to carry it away, he dragged a chair over to the corner and with shaky legs mounted it. As he reached the bust with feverish hands and clasped it, its weight proved too much for him. He staggered and fell from the chair, rolling head over heels on the floor, still clasping tightly to his breast his wooden image. Sullenly and shakily he rose to his feet ; and then reeled out of the room to wander later about the byways of Moscow and lose the encumbering bust in some gutter. That was the last view Isadora Duncan had of her poet and her husband, Sergey Alexandrovich Esenin."

But there was despair in his excesses. His buffoonery was that of a sentimental-romantic peasant boy who came too soon into the bedlam of a big city and was crushed by its grip. Unable either to adapt himself to it, or to rise above it and to escape, he wanted to drown his despair in the mire which he probably loathed yet without which he would have felt even more isolated and out of place, since his instincts and the very roots of his being had remained in another and totally different pattern of existence. He was born much too late to fit into the age and the conditions he lived in, let alone the chaotic turmoil of the period. A prey to his own sensitiveness, he would have, perhaps, collapsed sooner, had he not found a temporary refuge in cynicism, in alcohol and scandal. And when the trend of events took the direction of industrialism on a gigantic scale, Esenin—with his ideal of rural Arcadia—felt more dismayed than ever. Crushed by the depth of his own frustration, he arrived, in his tavern poems, at the conclusion that, together with him, everything else was doomed also. The following verses aptly convey what he meant :

The little thatched hut I was born in
Lies bare to the sky,
And in these crooked alleys of Moscow
I am fated to die.

No hope have I now of returning
To the fields where I played,
Of hearing the song of the poplar
As I lie in the shade.

The city is senile and dingy,
And drab, yet I love it !
The golden somnolent East
Is brooding above it.

And at night when the moon is a-shining
(A hell of a moon !)
I lurch through the slums till I come to
My favourite saloon.

There all the night through there is riot,
And babble and sin,
I read out my verses to harlots
And treat them to gin.

Still fiercer and quicker my heart beats,
This is all I can say:
"I am lost, you are lost, we are all lost,
I don't know the way."

The little thatched hut I was born in
Lies bare to the sky,
And in these crooked alleys of Moscow
*I am fated to die.**

In moods such as this Esenin called himself the "last of village poets" and predicted that rapid mechanisation of the land. which, according to him, was to destroy all the romance of patriarchal life he had known and loved in his boyhood:

I am the last of village poets;
A plank bridge croons but modest songs.
I celebrate the requiem mass
Of censer-swinging leafy birch.

The iron guest will soon appear
And pace the paths of azure fields,
His swarthy hand will snatch away
The oaten sheaves spilled out by dawn.

* Translated by R. M. Hewitt.

O hands, your touch is lifeless, strange,
These songs won't live within your reach.
And only ears of corn, like steeds,
Will grieve and mourn their master old.

And, dancing requiem dances, winds
Will suck their mournful quivering neighs.
The moon will strike its wooden hours
*And snore my twelfth and final hour.**

Provocative in his manners and in his verses, Esenin paraded, at times, words and expressions which are banished from civilised intercourse. As he could no longer invariably rely upon his inspiration, he often piled up images some of which were tiresomely laboured. Yet his tavern poems have a genuine tragic ring and produce, now and then, the effect of lived hallucinations.

V

IT WAS DURING THOSE YEARS OF RIOT AND SCANDAL that nostalgia for his lost and therefore poetically embellished Arcadia became particularly painful. One can feel it in his *Confessions of a Hooligan* (1920), and somewhat differently in his *Return Home* (1924), where the encroachment of the new Soviet village left little or no room for his old dreams.

* Translated by G. Reavey in *Soviet Literature* (Wishart).

Rain with arrows in a crowd
Has convulsed my home with cloud,
Mowed the blue bud from the land,
Trampled down the golden sand,
*Rain with arrows in a crowd.**

Even his sister, a fresh peasant girl, pored "as if it were a Bible," over Marx's *Capital*. The idyllic Russia was gone. All that she left behind was the nervousness of a transition period, alien to his simple peasant instincts. For, with all his puzzling ways, Esenin was much too simple for the age and the conditions he was compelled to live in. Having tasted of glory and adulation ; of riot and scandal ; of travels (together with Isadora Duncan) in America, Germany and France, he yet remained inwardly tied to the village—inert and "patriarchal" because of its very inertia. But while refusing to outgrow it, he suddenly saw himself outgrown and left behind by the new sovietised village which he did not want to accept. Hence his aimlessness and bewilderment. And as for his premature fame, it only unbalanced him like strong adulterated wine indulged in by a child.

Too sensitive and much too weak to face the unpleasant realities, he remained hanging in the air—a stranger to the world in which there was no room for his archaic dreams and ideals. So he took revenge upon life as well as upon himself through a kind of moral *harakiri*, and revelled as it were in his gradual self-destruction. It is true that during the last two

* Translated by C. M. Bowra. Op. cit.

years of his life he had a few quiet intervals, but it was the quiet of tiredness and of surrender to his own disgust. Even in those rare moments when he was inclined to "accept all without yearning for anything," he still yearned: for his squandered youth; for a different kind of life; for the rural Atlantis submerged by the Revolution. A last visit (after his parting from Isadora Duncan) to the haunts of his early years only made things worse. Instead of recovering his paradise lost, he felt that he was a walking anachronism—out of joint with everybody and everything, his native village included. All he could do was to translate his sorrow into lyrics, or else stifle it in riotous night life.

With regard to form he now underwent another change. Having abandoned the "imaginist" eccentricities, he chose for his model the lucid genius of Pushkin. Once more he sang in simple intimate strains. In his *Persian Themes* he even caught something of Pushkin's serene insouciance which lasted, however, only during his wanderings in the East. On his return home he was plunged into the former welter, but this time the gap between fancy and reality was steadily widening. It was no use drugging himself with wine, women and scandal. Besides, he already felt too tired for such expedients. At the age of thirty he was like an old man who had nothing to hope for, nothing to work for, nothing to look forward to. A victim of hypochondria, disgust and self-disgust, he saw only one way of escape and he took it. A juvenile melodramatic touch was lent to his death by the fact that he wrote his last poem in his own blood.

Such was the literary career of the poet whose personal fate was in a way symbolic of the transition period between the two Russias—the old and the new ; between the agricultural pattern of existence on the one hand, and the birth-pangs of the industrialised socialist society on the other. The inner conflict involved by this change found in Esenin a pathetic voice which, in its turn, appealed to thousands of readers and was responsible for his vogue during and immediately after the revolution. It was his pastoral nostalgia that found a ready response in all those contemporaries who regretted the passing away of the old rural Russia, and they consisted by no means of mere *kulaks*.

As it happens, each period has its own swan-song. The gentry period of Russian life found it in Turgenev's work ; the intelligentsia period—in Chekhov ; and the archaic peasant Russia—in Esenin. Suspended over the gulf of the vanishing past and the as yet much too complicated and therefore problematic future, he could not help reacting in the way he did. Suicide became only the last act of his own line of least resistance.

FOURTEEN

Vladimir Mayakovsky

I

APART FROM BEING THE MOST PROMINENT POET OF THE revolutionary period proper, Vladimir Mayakovsky is something of a landmark in Russian poetry as a whole. Like his rival, Sergey Esenin, he achieved both fame and notoriety before the cataclysm of 1917, yet the source from which he drew his inspiration was widely different from the one that appealed to the pastoral trend of Esenin. While Esenin clung to the pattern of the old peasant Russia, Mayakovsky was a hater of any settled patterns of existence, a breaker of rules and taboos. So instead of looking back to the past, he devoted his talent to the shaping of the future. He actually started his poetic career under the banner of futurism. But it would be wrong to lump the small futurist group of Russian poets together with the Italian futurists who had their heyday between 1910 and 1915. The Italian movement under that name, initiated and led by Marinetti, was a noisy reaction to the weight of too big a cultural heritage. An excess of humanistic tradition was felt to be a drawback, a brake, in an age of technique, of speed and machines. Consequently an attempt was made to ignore that tradition and to turn art itself into a glorification of the mechanical values of life. Marinetti's revulsion from Italy's over-rich humanistic past was so complete indeed that he tried to drag, with a hysterical impetus, not only literature but also painting and the plastic arts from the plane of culture to that of an up-to-date technical civilisation, imbued with the spirit of a Darwinian struggle for existence and the survival of the fittest. It was Marinetti who anticipated (*via* d'Annunzio and a semi-digested Nietzsche) all the elements of fascism and of the "dynamic" mailed fist. What that tendency was like can be gathered from the *Initial Manifesto*, issued during the exhibition of Italian futurist art in London, in 1912. Here are some of its pronouncements:

"Literature has hitherto glorified thoughtful immobility, ecstasy and sleep ; we shall extol aggressive movement, feverish insomnia, the double quick step, the somersault, the box on the ear, the fist cuff.

"We wish to glorify War—the only health-giver of the world—militarism, patriotism ; the destructive arm of the Anarchist, the beautiful ideas that kill, contempt for woman.

"We wish to destroy the museums, the libraries ; we fight against moralism, feminism and all opportunistic and utilitarian meannesses.

"Set fire to the shelves of libraries! Divert the courses of the canals to flood the cellars of the museums! Oh! may the glorious canvases drift helplessly! Seize pickaxes and hammers! Sap the foundations of the venerable cities!

"We stand upon the summit of the world and once more cast our challenge to the stars!"

The frothy rhetoric of these sentences speaks for itself. A psychologist can easily detect in it the fury of a vain but sterile mind, anxious to lay the blame for its own sterility on the excessive culture of the past. In Russia, however, where there was little evidence of an over-ripe cultural heritage, the position as well as the task of the futurists was essentially different. A new poetic technique, more appropriate to our modern pace and manner of life, was—as in Italy and elsewhere—one of its aims. But otherwise the overwhelming tradition of the past was not one of culture, but of autocracy and political oppression. This means that a fight for the future had to start with a fight against those evils. Hence the curious paradox that while in Italy futurism degenerated into a staunch supporter of fascist oppression, in Russia it switched over to the Revolution, which indeed found its principal bard in Mayakovsky.

II

IT GOES WITHOUT SAYING THAT THE TECHNICAL innovations introduced into poetry by Mayakovsky were directed above all against symbolism, especially against its "feminine," or perhaps effeminate, characteristics. He demanded a clearer, more concrete and at the same time more robust and warlike poetry —a poetry which would not shrink from any harshness of thought and expression. Hence his challenge—

My words
are not used
to caressing ears ;
nor titillate
with semi-obscenities
maiden ears
hidden in hair so innocent.
I open on parade
my pages of fighters,
pass in review
their lineal front.
My verses stand
in lead-heavy letters
ready for death
*and for deathless glory.**

The small group of the Russian futurists, led by Mayakovsky and consisting of lower middle-class bohemian *déclassés*, thus started their activities in a warlike mood. Defying the traditional public taste, they tried to revolutionise Russian prosody, word-formation, syntax, and made some interesting excursions (especially in the case of Velemir Khlebnikov) into the realm of the so-called pristine word. Some

* Translated by George Reavey in *Soviet Literature* (Wishart).

members of the group even invented a "translogical" language of their own, based on the suggestiveness of sound and rhythm, going much farther in this respect than, say, James Joyce during his last period. Mayakovsky's experiments were less eccentric and more solid. In his attempt to create a new type of poetry designed especially for the platform, he freed the verse from metre and based it on intonation. His rhythmic system was thus divorced from the old lyrical melody. He was concerned with the dynamic and dramatic value of single words instead, which now tended to become independent units. This involved a new rôle on the part of pauses, inflections, and also punctuation. The so-called spatial punctuation—with its peculiar pattern of printed words extending over the whole page—had been started by the symbolists, especially by Andrey Bely and Alexeỳ Remizov. But Mayakovsky adopted it for his own purposes and brought it to perfection.

Having abandoned the former melodious and symmetrical verse, he proceeded to work out his loud and essentially rhetorical platform-technique by means of which a poem was often reduced to the equivalent of a poster or a cartoon—with such a mixture of planes as to achieve a maximum of *striking* expressiveness. In contrast to the symbolists, who were concerned with the inner reality, he concentrated on an intensified rendering of external things as such. Hence the harsh "palpability" of his poetic language, of his metaphors, similes, unexpected parallelisms and associations. He indulged in dissonances in rhyme and also in his invariable staccato manner. As if taking tips from Nekrasov, he continued to depoetise poetry—through slang, through street and tavern-jargon, while making deliberate use of hyperbolisms on a colossal scale. (In one of his poems he depicts himself walking about with the sun as his monocle and holding Napoleon on a leash like a terrier.) Yet Mayakovsky's depoetised verse tends to be poetry of a new and forcefully suggestive kind. The *Prologue* to one of his longer poems may serve as illustration.

Your thought
that muses on a sodden brain,
as a fattened lackey on a green couch,
I shall taunt with my heart's bloody tatters ;
satiate *my insolent, caustic contempt.*
Not a single grey hair streaks my soul,
not a trace of grandfatherly fondness !
I shake the world with the might of my voice,
and stalk—handsome,
twenty-two year old.

Gentle souls !
You fiddle sweet loves,
but the crude club their love on a drum.
Try, as I do, and wrench
yourself inside out and be just engulfing lips !

Come and be lessoned—
prim graduates of the angel league,
from boudoirs lisping in cambric !

You who tranquilly finger your lips
as cooks page a cookery book.

. . . .

I do not believe in flowery Nice!
I sing once again
men crumpled as hospital beds
*and women as trite as a proverb.**

Colloquial bonhomie, combined with satire, parody, and a grotesque mythology of his own in which a mixture of the trivial and the comically grandiose plays the principal part, is one of Mayakovsky's frequent devices. Among his Parisian poems, for example, there is one in which he chats with the Eiffel Tower, trying to make it leave "this Paris of prostitutes, poets, bourse, the gap-yawning boulevards" and emigrate to Soviet Russia where it would presumably feel more at ease, and ends with the promise to get it a visa. Or take this *Most Extraordinary Adventure*, which "happened to me, Vladimir Mayakovsky, at the Rumyantsev Summerhouse, Mount Akula, Pushkino, on the Yaroslav Railway." On a hot July day, the poet—in a joking mood—invited the Sun himself to come down for a while and have a cup of tea with him. But the Sun took the invitation seriously and began to descend—

Coming of his own free will,
Striding with great flaming rays
Across the field
And down the hill.

* Translated by George Reavey. Op. cit.

I don't want to seem afraid,
So I take a few steps back.
Now his eyes are in the garden,
He's coming up the garden path.
Through the windows
And the doors,
Through every crack
In the walls and the floors
The great flaming bulk
Of the sun's body pours
And pours.
And a very big breath he draws,
And in a deep voice makes this exclamation :
"I have turned my fires back you see
For the first time since creation.
I heard you calling me.
So here I am.
Come on, you poet, hurry up with that tea,
Come on, and I want some jam !"
Tears were pouring out of my eyes,
With the heat.
I was quite unsteady.
But I got to work
And soon had the samovar ready.
"All right I said,
Come on, old Shiner, and take a seat."

It must have been the devil
Who gave me the cheek
To yell out that invitation.
There I sat sadly

On the edge of the bench
In the greatest trepidation.
You see I was very scared
That things would turn out badly.
But from the sun
A strange brilliance flared
And I soon forgot
My shyness.
And gradually I got into conversation
With his celestial highness.

I began to chat
Of this and that,
I was calling him, "old boy,"
And I clapped him on the back.
And the Sun said: "See here,
You and I, comrade,
Are a pair, that's clear.
Come, poet, come with me,
We'll soar and we'll sing,
And defeat the world's dingy curses,
Over all that trash my beams I'll pour
You'll flood it with your verses!"

. . . .

To shine—
No nonsense, I say,
That's the sun's slogan,
*And it is mine.**

* Translated by V. de Sola Pinto. The poem is quoted with considerable omissions.

VLADIMIR MAYAKOVSKY

III

WHATEVER SUBJECT MAYAKOVSKY TOOK ON, HE FILLED it with his own vitality, as well as with his sonorous voice, which seemed to be created expressly for the platform and mass meetings. In handling the word as such he certainly had no equals. One of the contemporary Russian critics, Roman Jakobson, goes so far to say that the "word of Mayakovsky is qualitative and different from anything that preceded him in the Russian verse, and no matter how many genetic links we may try to establish—the pattern of his poetry remains profoundly original and revolutionary." But if so, it is the more interesting to watch how and why he eventually dedicated the whole of his talent to the cause of the working classes and of the new socialist era. Not that such a thing happened all at once, or that there were no other side to his being. On the contrary, it is enough to compare his poetry before 1917 with the verses he wrote after the Revolution in order to see that there were at least two Mayakovskys whose interrelations were very much dependent on the peculiar circumstances of his life.

Born in 1893 in the Caucasus, where his father was a forest-ranger, he did not know poverty until 1906, about which year we read in his brief autobiography: "Father died. End of prosperity. After father's funeral we had three roubles left. Instinctively, feverishly, we sold our chairs and tables. Moved to Moscow. Why? Not even acquaintances there."*

* Translated by Herbert Marshall in *Mayakovsky* (Pilot Press).

In Moscow he settled, together with his mother and his two sisters, to a precarious semi-proletarian existence. In 1908 he became a member of the Russian Social-Democratic Party, was arrested, and spent eleven months in prison, where he started writing verse. The same year is marked by the following passage: "Entered School of Painting, Sculpture and Architecture. Only place that did not ask for a certificate of good conduct. Worked well. Was amazed to find imitators petted and original minds badgered. By revolutionary instinct stood up for the badgered ones."

In the Art School Mayakovsky developed his talent for drawing posters—an occupation which he continued (also in his poems) until his death in 1930. It was here that he met another dissatisfied youth, David Burlyuk, who appreciated Mayakovsky the poet before any of his verses were published. An amusing example of the shock-tactics this friend employed in his interests occurred once after Mayakovsky had read to him, for the first time, some of his poems. "In the morning, Burlyuk, introducing me to someone, trumpeted: 'Don't you know him? My genius friend. Famous poet Mayakovsky.' I tried to stop him. Burlyuk was adamant. Leaving me, he bellowed: 'Now write or you will make me look a regular fool.' "

Although a poor man himself, Burlyuk gave Mayakovsky half-a-rouble daily so that he could write poetry without starving. Before long he introduced him to two other youngsters who, together with them, formed the nucleus of Russian futurism. But let us quote Mayakovsky's reminiscences once again. "Khlebnikov in Moscow. His quiet genius was at that time completely overshadowed by the roaring David. Here, too, was Kruchonykh—futurist, jesuit of words. After a few lyrical nights we gave birth to a joint manifesto. David collected the material, copied it, christened the manifesto and published *A Slap at Public Taste*."* This juvenile venture was followed by a series of lectures and scandals in the two capitals and also in some bigger cities in the provinces. Then the year 1913 was suddenly marked by the brief "tragedy in verse," *Vladimir Mayakovsky*, which was actually performed (by amateurs) in one of the parks at St. Petersburg.

IV

AS THE NARCISSISTIC TITLE INDICATES, THIS WORK IS a "grandiose" self-dramatisation, natural enough in a youth of twenty and a gate-crasher in the temple of fame into the bargain. At the same time it is Mayakovsky's own equivalent of *Une Saison en Enfer*—with the world as its setting and with the humans teeming around like "bells on the fool's cap of God." It is also his first display of defiance born of despair. Like Gogol, Mayakovsky too (to use his own words) "crucified on a cross of laughter his own tormented groan." But whereas Gogol's method reminds one of Hogarth, that of Mayakovsky is more like a mixture

* Translated by Herbert Marshall. Op. cit.

of Picasso with the wildest fantasies of H. Bosch. Among his *dramatis personae* there actually appear (as allegorical accessories to Mayakovsky himself) an old man—thousands of years old—with dried-up black cats; a man without an eye and one foot; a man without an ear; a man without a head—all this in the same "expressionist" poster-like style which he adopted also in his next three longer poems: *A Cloud in Trousers*, *The Backbone Flute*, and *War and Peace*.

The original title of the first of these three works was *The Thirteenth Apostle*, but it was not passed by the censor. It is a vociferous poetic document in which, as in a fugue, Mayakovsky's frustrated personal love is combined with his social indignation raised to the point of rebellion against the world-order itself. In a preface to the second edition of this work (in 1918) he referred to it as a catechism of present-day art, but this can only be applied to it in a negative, destructive sense. "Down with your kind of love! Down with your kind of art! Down with your system of life! Down with your religion!" Such are the slogans of its four parts. Its "colossal" metaphors are deliberately heavy; and however strange it may appear at times on the surface, the inner association of the externally incongruous things is there. For all its extravagances, this is a most effective work, in which Mayakovsky's pathos of despair is expressed by an adequate new tonality and a new technique.

This pathos is even more intense in his *Backbone Flute*, which is inwardly connected with the previous poem, or rather with the previous two poems. In the teeth of all the rules of Marinetti's futurism, the tragedy of his own love is again one of Mayakovsky's *leitmotifs*, alternating or else running parallel with his social-political theme. Here his unrequited passion is treated as a curse, a punishment, torment and self-torment, the only result of which is inner devastation. Such a note, aggravated by a definite foreboding of his own tragic end, prevails also in his anti-bourgeois poem, *Man* (1917), whereas in *War and Peace* (written, in 1916, under the impact of the first World War) the social momentum is stronger—probably under the influence of Gorky in whose periodical, *The Annals*, he wrote at the time. Mayakovsky gave here another poetic poster, interpreting the world in terms of the blood-stained arena in the Roman Colosseum. Anti-militaristic in the extreme, it ends with the dream of a better and united world, inhabited by a new species of man.

And such day has dawned
That Andersen's tales
Were crawling at its feet like puppies.

V

DURING THE WHOLE OF THAT PERIOD MAYAKOVSKY'S source of inspiration was above all his unhappy love* which he "clubbed on a drum," with the chaotic world around as its background. He was a revolutionary by

* He was in love with a woman (Mme Brik) who was married to one of his friends and early publishers.

temperament rather than by any definite aims or convictions. Yet when the Revolution of 1917 broke out, it provided a supra-personal aim and outlet which he adopted the more eagerly because he was not rooted either in the intelligentsia tradition like Blok and Bely, or in the peasant tradition like Esenin and Klyuyev. He embraced the tasks of the Revolution in their entirety and became the poet of the rising masses—even if his voice and manner were often those of a poetic "boss" rather than a servant of the Revolution. But the very fervour with which he now voiced its cause may have been prompted by his wish to "crush under foot" the melody of his personal love-drama which had only been pushed aside rather than sublimated. Hence the over-loud character of his propaganda poems, beginning with his play, *Mystery-Bouffe* (1918, a revised edition in 1921).

This deliberately crude parody of the old mystery-plays is called by Mayakovsky a "heroic, epic and satirical picture of our epoch." It is done in the style of a spectacular cartoon and, like all cartoons, it lacks depth, however amusing the very coarseness of its surface. The poet's familiar patting of the cosmos passes here into music-hall jokes and blasphemies about God, and the whole allegory is typical of the author's attempt to "restore to the theatre its spectacular character and to turn the stage itself into a platform." The figures include the Unclean ones (the proletarians), the Clean ones (the bourgeoisie), mixed up with God, the angels, and the devils. After the flood has destroyed the old earth, the Unclean rebel against the Clean ones and relegate them to Hell. Then they visit the heavenly Paradise which does not impress them at all. In fact, they leave it with scorn and go back to the ravaged earth which they want to transform into the Promised Land of happiness, of plenty and of universal comfort. The finale is similar to the one in Mayakovsky's *War and Peace*, but this time the stress is laid on the working class which—through the triumph of socialism, work and technique—has become the ruler of the world. It all ends, poster-like, with the paraphrased *Internationale*:

All memory of the past shall perish;
The bourgeois rule is crushed and lost.
The earth we hold and aye shall cherish.
We, soldiers of the toilers' host.
From fields and factories ascend,
Come from the towns both great and small.
The world is ours from end to end,
*We who were nought, today are all.**

Mystery-Bouffe is Mayakovsky's counterpart and polar contrast of Esenin's *Inonia*. He would hear of no idyllic peasant paradise on earth. Nor is he afraid of the machine, of technique, provided that man shall be its master and not its slave. It is all rather simplified, yet in the years of Civil War it must have served its purpose well. No less simplified is his long allegorical poem, "150,000,000". Written in 1919, it represents the moujik Ivan in a single combat with President

* Translated by G. R. Noyes and Alex. Kaun (Appleton).

Wilson—the champion of capitalism. The issue of the duel is, of course, a foregone conclusion.

Such loud and poster-like poetry required no strain on the part of the audiences in so far as it was offered with the flavour of smart journalism. The bulk of Mayakovsky's work after 1917 is actually a deliberate mixture of the two. Even his travel poems (1924-25) about France, Mexico and America are journalistic *feuilletons* in verse—full of quick observations, irony and political harangues. "In my work I am consciously becoming a newspaper man," Mayakovsky said at a time when he was pouring out countless propaganda limericks, rhymed slogans, and "agitkas" or agit-verses (his favourite genre), exhorting the Soviet citizens to perform their daily tasks and duties. He also asserted that "meetings, speeches, front-line limericks, one-day agit-prop playlets, the living radio-voice and the slogan flashing by on the trams—are all equal and sometimes valuable examples of poetry. To crown it all, he eventually defined his own verses as Com-Party poems and did not mind calling himself an "agitator, loud-speaker-in-chief." Here is an extract from his "agitka" *Hands off China* (1927):

War,
daughter of imperialism,
stalks,
a spectre through the world.
Workers roar: Hands off China!—
Hey, Macdonald,
don't meddle
in leagues and muddle speeches.

Back, dreadnoughts!
Hands off China!—
In the embassy quarters
kings meticulously
sit, weaving a web of intrigues.
We'll brush away the cobweb.
*Hands off China!**

VI

SUCH WAS THE CHARACTER OF MAYAKOVSKY'S POETRY (or whatever you call it) when the social-political element prevailed in it. Yet even his loudest voice was not loud enough to suppress in the long run that personal dilemma of his which he had tried to eliminate, or at least to silence. It kept troubling him, again and again, even during his most active propaganda period. In his poem *I Love* (1922), for example, he confessed—

In others I know the heart's abode
is in the bosom as we all know.
But on me
anatomy has run amok,
I am nothing but heart
tingling all over.

A year later another poem, *About That*, reminiscent

* Translated by George Reavey in *Soviet Literature* (Wishart).

of his pre-war poetry (especially of *The Backbone Flute*), contained the following motif:

> *"He" and "she" is my ballad.*
> *The terrible thing is that "he" is I*
> *and that "she" is mine.*

The constructive years that came after the Civil War was over, were inspiring enough to fill him with social enthusiasm to the exclusion (a temporary one) of disturbing personal problems. That period was responsible for his longest and best propaganda poem, *Vladimir Ilyich Lenin* (1924), on the occasion of Lenin's death. Despite its detailed passages about Marx etc., the poem reads like a paean to the Revolution and its leader whom, with a sudden flair for hero-worship, Mayakovsky relegates to the sphere of the great historical symbols.

> *He is earthly—*
> *but not of those*
> *whose nose*
> *delves only into*
> *their own little sty.*
> *He grasped the earth*
> *whole,*
> *all at one go,*
> *saw that*
> *which lay hidden*
> *in time.*

And in his diatribe against the modern super-capitalist as seen from Soviet Russia, Mayakovsky comes to the characteristic conclusion:

You can't
jump over him,
no how you dodge past,
Only one way out—
*explode!**

Between his propaganda poem, *Very Good* (1927), commemorating the tenth anniversary of the Revolution, and his personal confession, *At the Top of My Voice*, written in 1930 (that is, in the year of his suicide), Mayakovsky finished two satirical comedies, *The Bedbug* and *The Bathhouse.* The first is a "fantastic" satire—in nine pictures—on the eternal Philistine who emerged in many a Soviet citizen during the NEP period. We see a drunken NEP wedding, in the course of which a fire breaks out and burns all the revellers to death. Fifty years later one of them is resurrected (exactly as he was) by a special scientific method and proves to be such a mean and vulgar insect in human form as to cause regular panic. *The Bathhouse*, in six acts—"with a circus and a display of fire-works"—is a grotesque buffoonery directed against the bureaucratic careerists in the new Soviet State—a tendency which was welcomed during the party purge in 1929. In this case the "fantastic" element is provided by a time-machine which can transfer one into the future, and during one of such journeys the principal character (a cut-and-dried Soviet bureaucrat)

* Translated by Herbert Marshall. Op. cit.

is left behind together with his piled-up luggage. None of these works contains as much as a hint of the poet's personal secret. But in one of his last poems, *At the Top of My Voice*, the social and the personal motifs are mingled, once again, in such a significant manner that the only thing to do is to quote this extract from its beginning:

Highly respected
comrade posterity,
grubbing
in our present-day
petrified dirt,
studying the darkness of our generation,
You,
it may be, will inquire about me,
And
it may be that one
of your erudite scholars,
Cutting short with his learning
the stream of questions,
will say: Once there lived
a boiling hot singer,
a violent enemy of cold water.
Now Professor,
take off your optical bicycle,
I'll tell you in person
about my times
and about myself:
I was a sanitary man
and a watercarrier,

I was mobilised,
called up by the Revolution,
I went to the Front
from the lordly estate
Of Poetry—
a capricious old lady.

. . . .

Yet I'm
utterly fed up
with propaganda :
Yes I'd have liked
to strum
love songs to you,
They bring in good money
and they're delightful.
But I
conquered myself
and stamped
On the throat of my own song.
So listen here,
comrade posterity,
Listen to an agitator
*a wild bawling ranter.**

The last few lines have often been interpreted as a proof of Mayakovsky's disappointment in Revolution, which is obviously nonsense. They prove only one thing : that his enthusiastic work for the Revolution was not enough to save him from the complications of his intimate personal dilemma. But if he deliberate-

* Translated by V. de Sola Pinto.

ly chose to flee from it, to "stamp on the throat" of his own song, then even his revolutionary activities looked like escapism from himself, whether he was aware of it or not. Unable either to solve or else to crush his personal dilemma in his work for the bigger social cause, he must have been haunted by the idea of suicide even while writing some of his most spirited "agit-verses." The irony of it all was that he committed suicide at a time when he was universally regarded as the embodiment of socialist optimism. Worse—he gave away his secret in his jotting of a farewell letter by this simple statement: "For me there are no outlets."

VII

EACH HISTORICAL EPOCH CONFORMS TO THE TREND and pattern of life and, consequently, of art provided by the values of the dominant social group. So it is natural to assume that the new epoch inaugurated by the Soviet Union should gradually work out its own pattern of art and literature—anticipated by socialist realism and particularly by the writings of Mayakovsky. It is, perhaps, still too early to assess Mayakovsky's place in Russian literature, although one thing remains clear: he made a brave attempt to revolutionise not only the technique but the very role of poetry. One of the outstanding Soviet poets, Boris Pasternak, does not hesitate to ascribe to him (in his *Safe Conduct*) the greatest poetic destiny. "Whenever afterwards our generation expressed itself dramatically, lending its voice to a poet, be it Esenin, Selvinsky, or Tsvetayeva, in precisely those ties which bound them to each other and to their generation, that is, in their appeal from their times to the universe, the echo of Mayakovsky's consanguineous note was heard. I say nothing regarding masters such as Tikhonov and Aseyev, because I am linking myself to this dramatic tendency."*

Pasternak, who is a chamber poet *par excellence*, obviously refers here above all to Mayakovsky's personal poetry. But as for his propaganda poems proper, the question still remains open in how far they are poetry if measured by our existing standards. To call them so wholeheartedly would mean to revise our definition of poetry in more respects than one. As though sensing the thorny side of this dilemma, the younger generation launched (especially after 1937) the slogan "back to Pushkin," as a corrective. While making use of all the technical innovations introduced by Mayakovsky, the younger poets aim once again at that lucid and restrained simplicity which was typical of Pushkin. Moreover, "back to Pushkin" means also a return to the broad, tolerant humanism represented by him.

The convergence between socialism and humanism is, beyond doubt, among the vital issues of our time. So vital indeed that, unless the new socialist society is founded on a broad humanistic basis—with its respect for individual rights and liberties, then socialism itself

* From *Boris Pasternak. The Collected Works* (Lindsay Drummond).

may become totalitarian. And totalitarianism from the left can in the end be as ruthless as that from the right. It is for this reason that the development of Soviet literature is important also as a pointer to the state and the trends of present-day Russian consciousness. But we need not be apprehensive. In Soviet Russia, literature, whatever its ups and downs, is a more vital factor of life than it ever was in the past. And as in the past, it is likely to continue its social and humanising rôle without thereby forfeiting its high artistic standards.

Conclusion

IF PUSHKIN IS A GREAT LANDMARK AT THE BEGINNING of modern Russian literature, Mayakovsky (a much lesser man) forms a suitable transition to something new yet inextricably bound up with such a crisis of Russian history and of Russian consciousness as the one represented by the cataclysm of 1917. A century of intense activities, of quest and travail was relegated by that cataclysm to the past, but the values of literature remained. Whatever social, political and psychological changes may have taken place, the essential literary continuity has been preserved without any unbridgeable gaps between the old and the new. Even Mayakovsky's futurism made no radical difference in this respect. New poetic, technical and ideological devices merged and are still merging with the creative heritage of the past in order to work out gradually a literature in accordance with the social-political pattern which resulted from the revolution and is now voicing the need of a general integration of the individual and society, of culture and life.

This is the principal reason why a knowledge of the period between Pushkin and Mayakovsky is the best introduction to that literature which came after 1917. Moreover, no one can properly understand some of the deeper psychological roots of the greatest upheaval in modern history unless he knows something of that crisis of Russian consciousness which reached its blind-alley in Chekhov, Andreyev, Blok and Esenin. And whatever the future verdict of such transition figures as Gorky and Mayakovsky may be, they will be remembered as men who helped Russian literature to turn the corner at a time when the very existence of Russia was at stake.

INDEX

INDEX

INDEX